MANDALA SEASONS

ADULT COLORING BOOK

FRUIT & FLOWERS

BOOK 1

PRODUCED BY

Maya Necalli

&

ART THERAPY DESIGNS

INTRODUCTION

Art Therapy Designs presents unique theme-based mandala collections inspired by various world cultures and the natural world. This is the first book in the *Mandala Seasons: Fruit & Flowers* series.

This coloring book contains 45 floral patterns presented as single-sided pages to help preserve each illustration.

The designs range from easy to high difficulty with the latter half being the most difficult.

Feel free to begin wherever you'd like!

Coloring is a form of art therapy, a creative calming technique that aids in de-stressing and relaxation.

Our therapeutic activity book is designed for grownups but suitable for all advanced children and teens.

Enjoy!

NOTE: Cover image can be found at the beginning.

SPECIAL OFFERS

Visit our Facebook page to get free designs and find out when new coloring books are available!

Go to: www.facebook.com/ArtTherapyDesigns

You can also win freebies and keep up with new releases by joining our newsletter (see Facebook page).

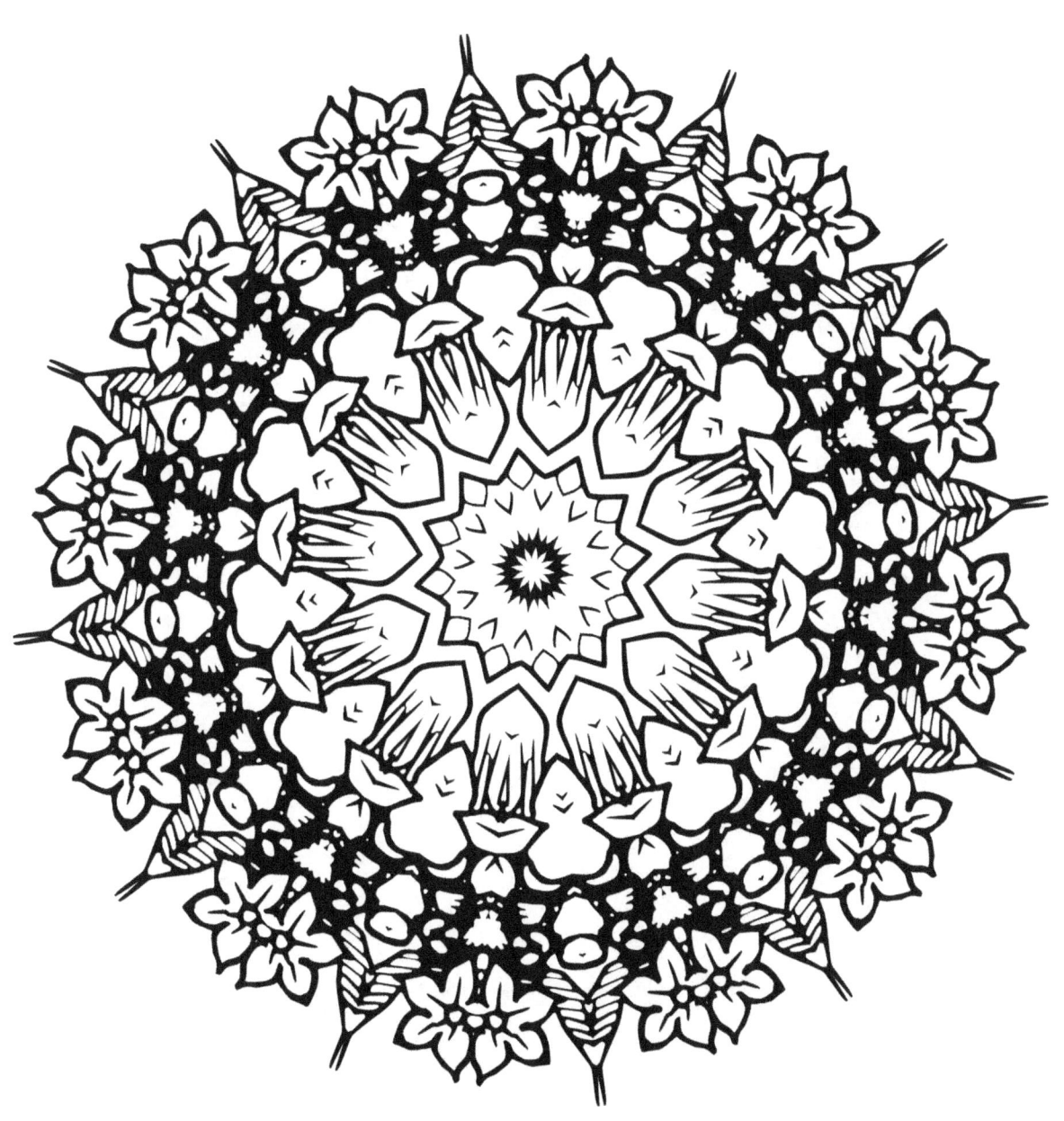

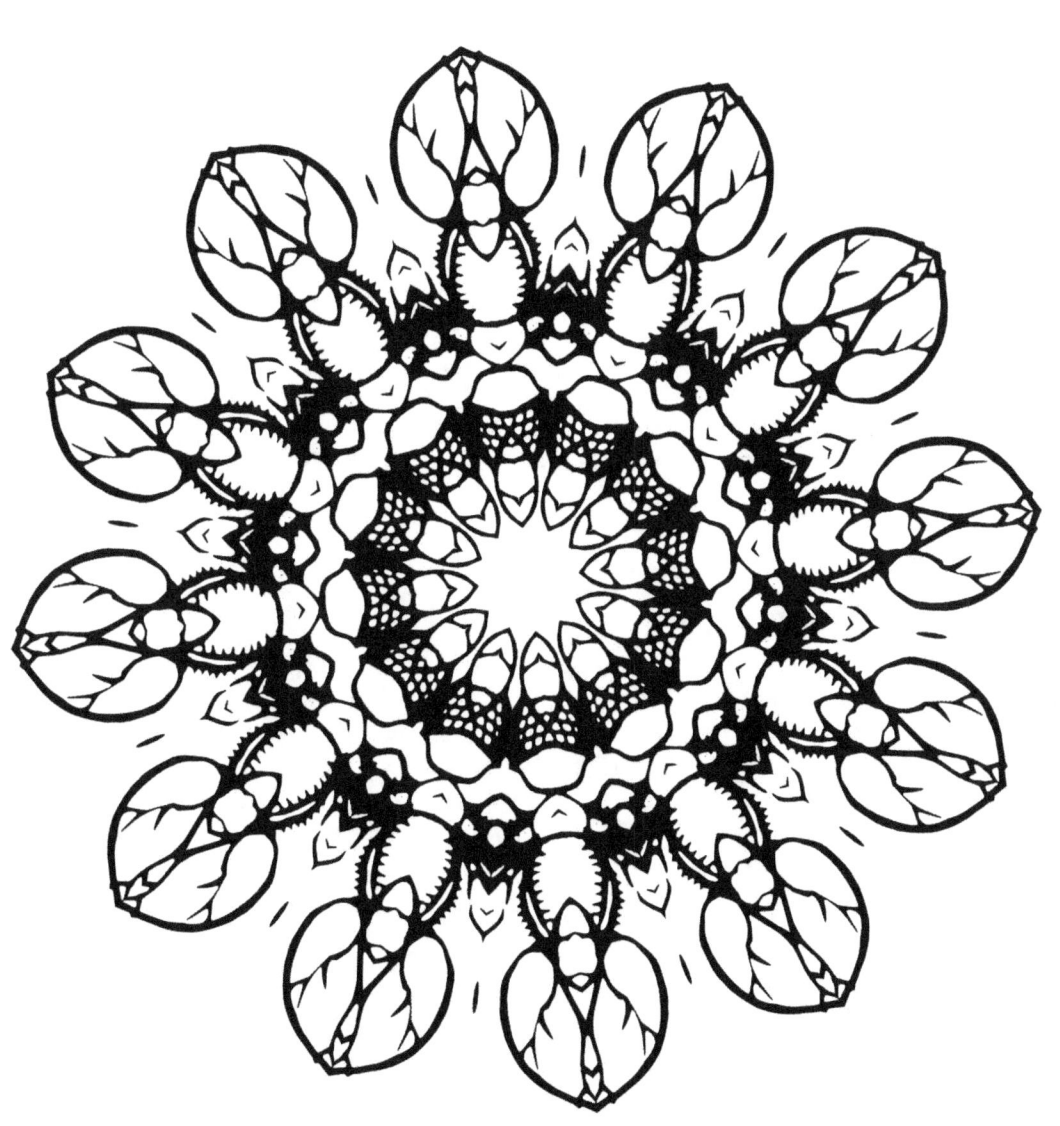

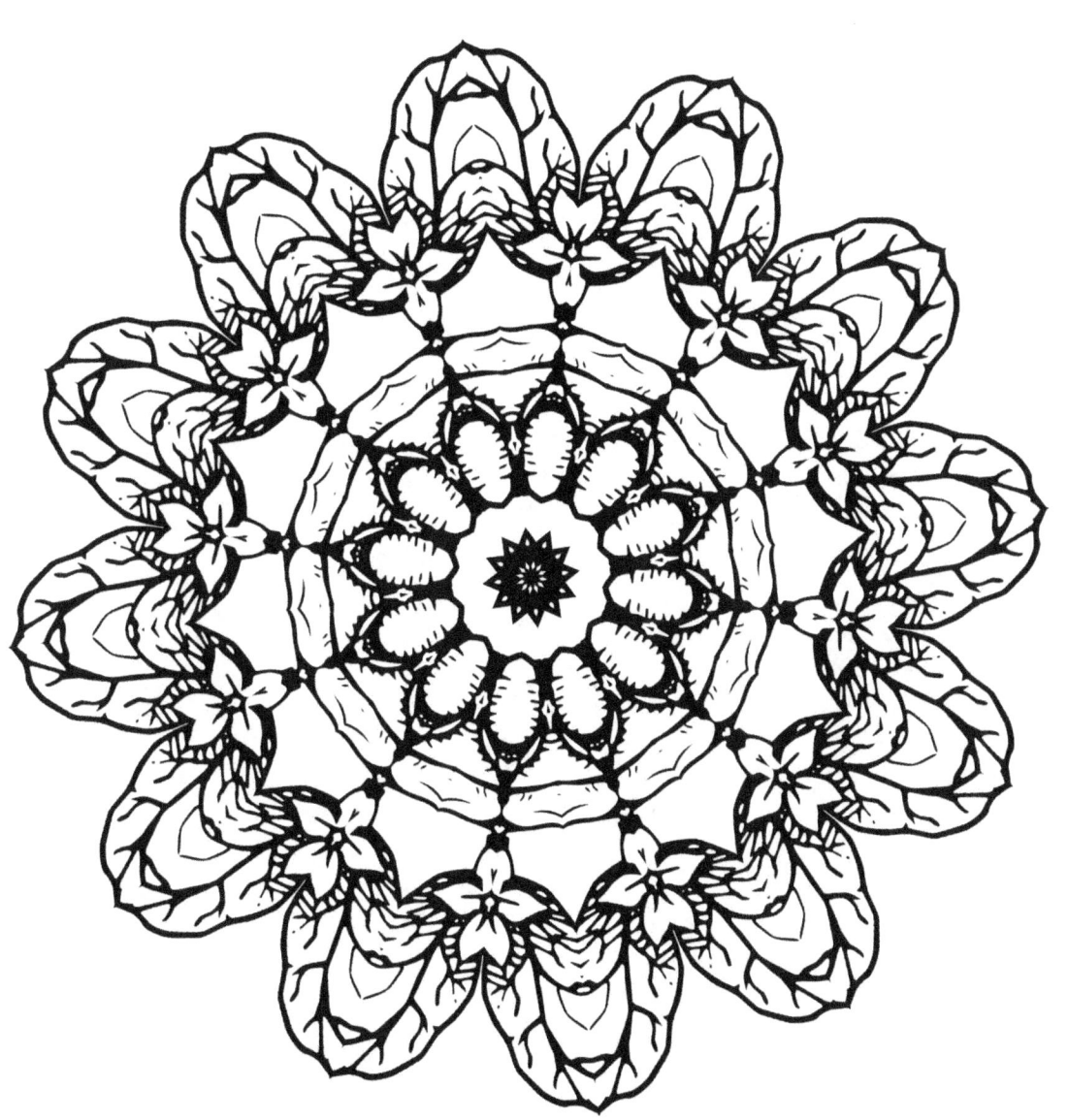

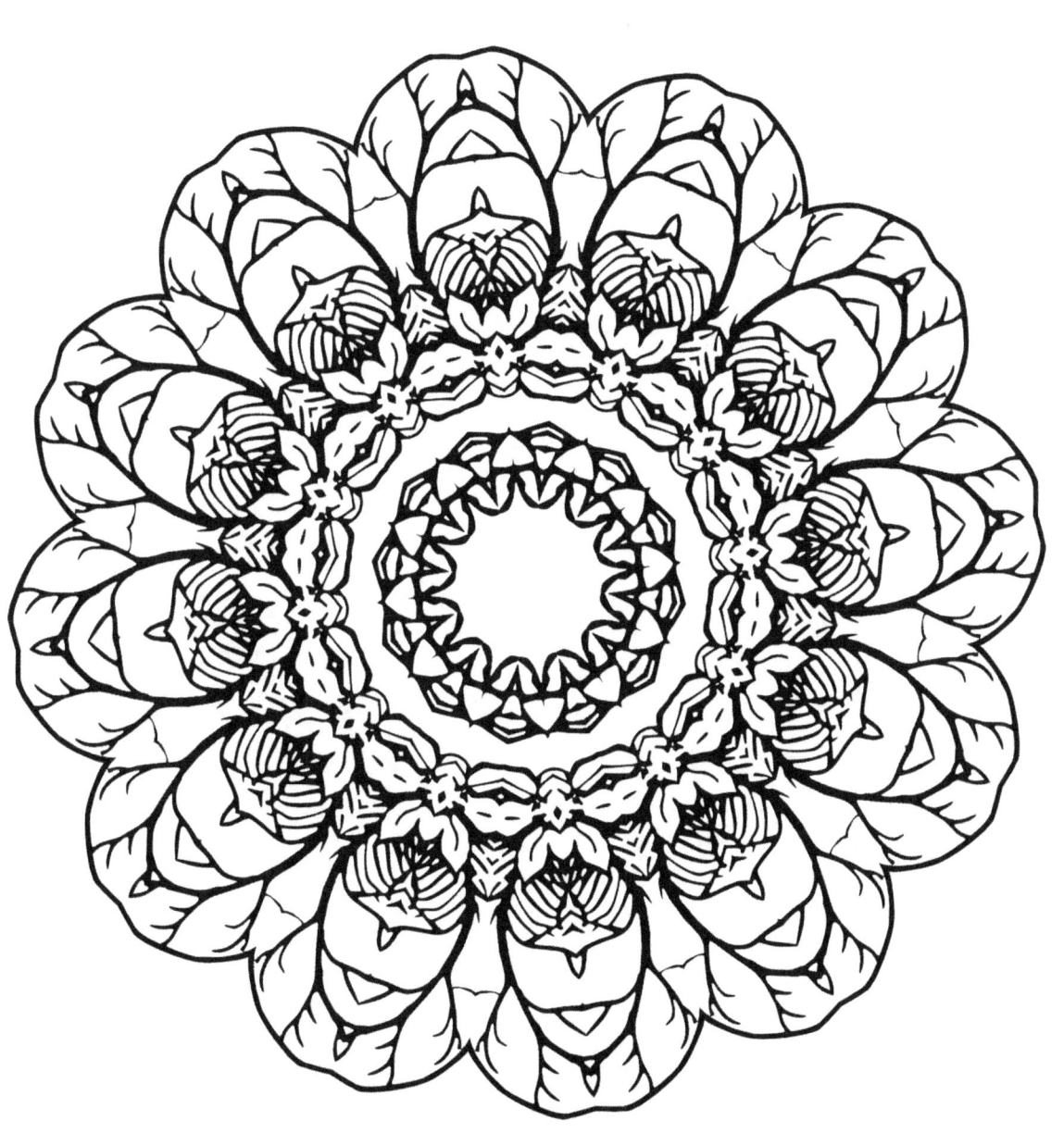

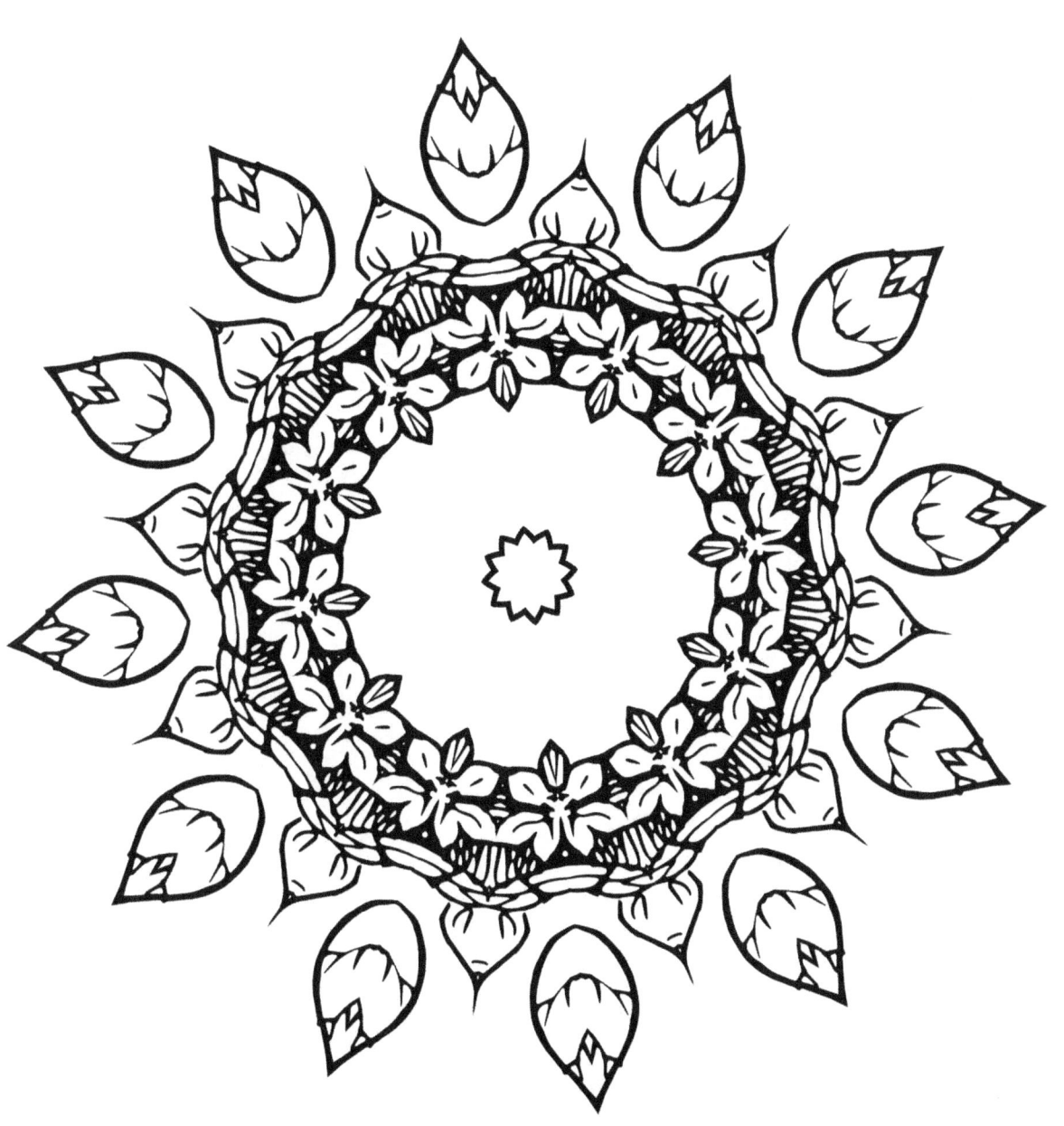

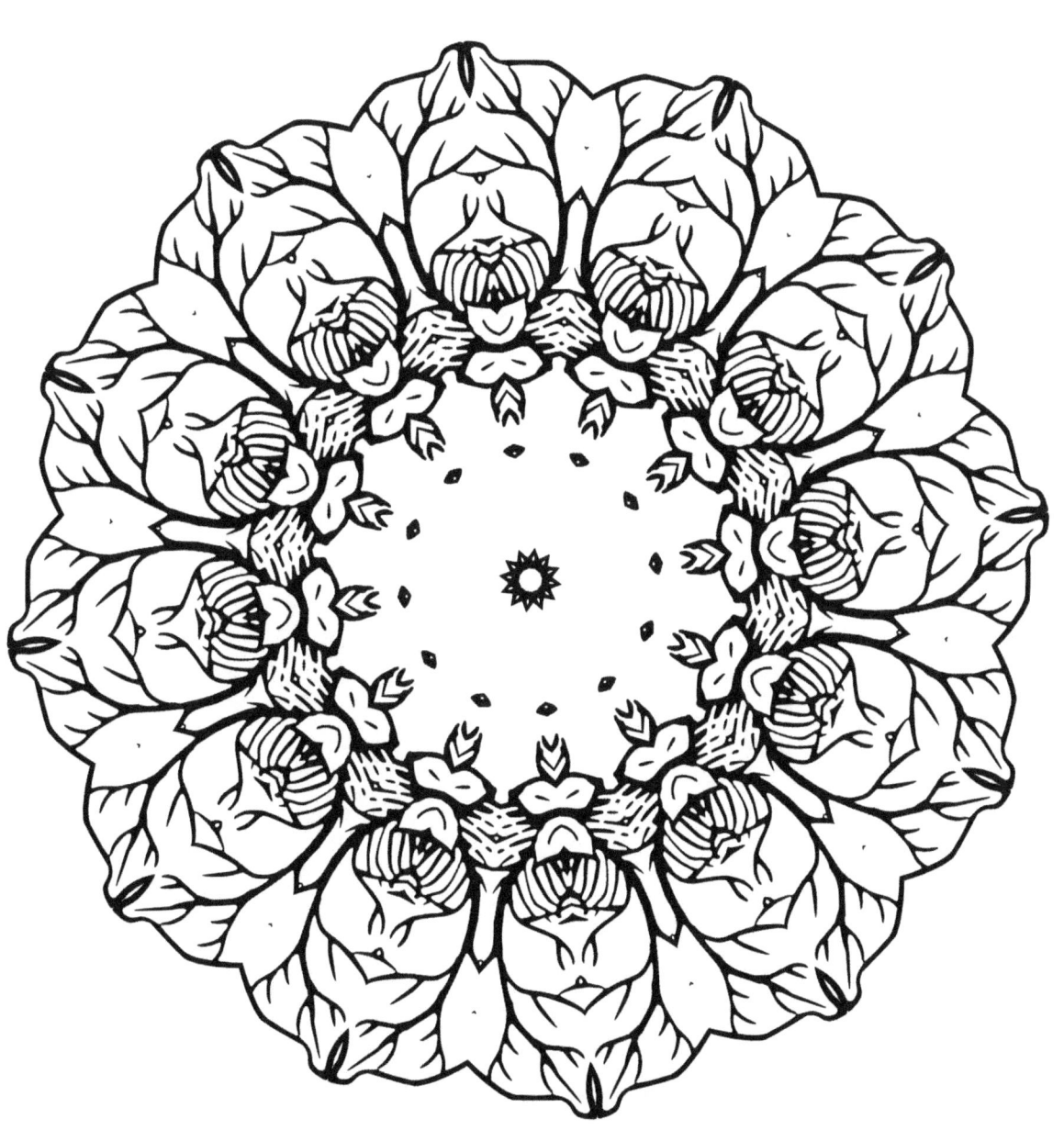

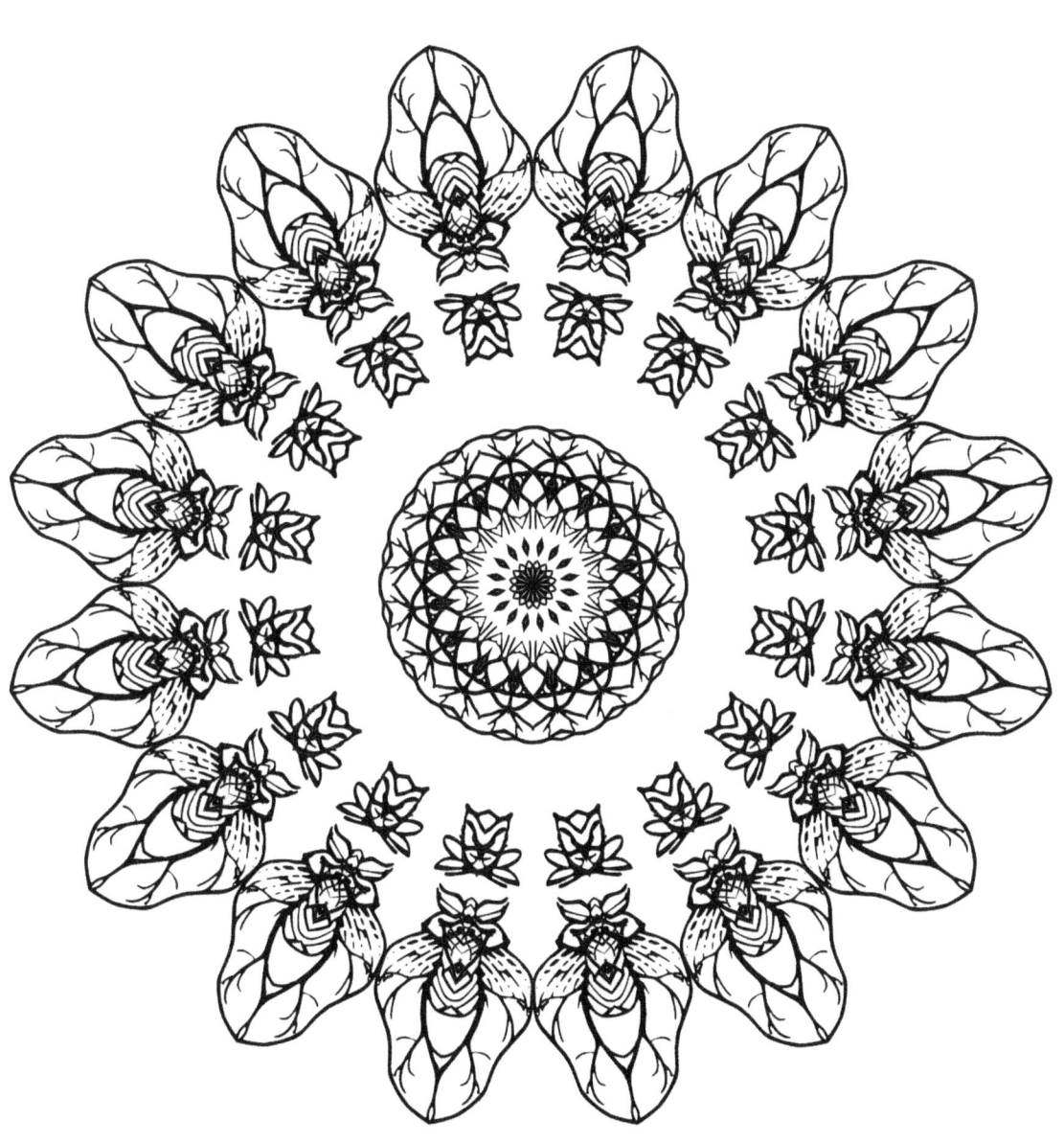

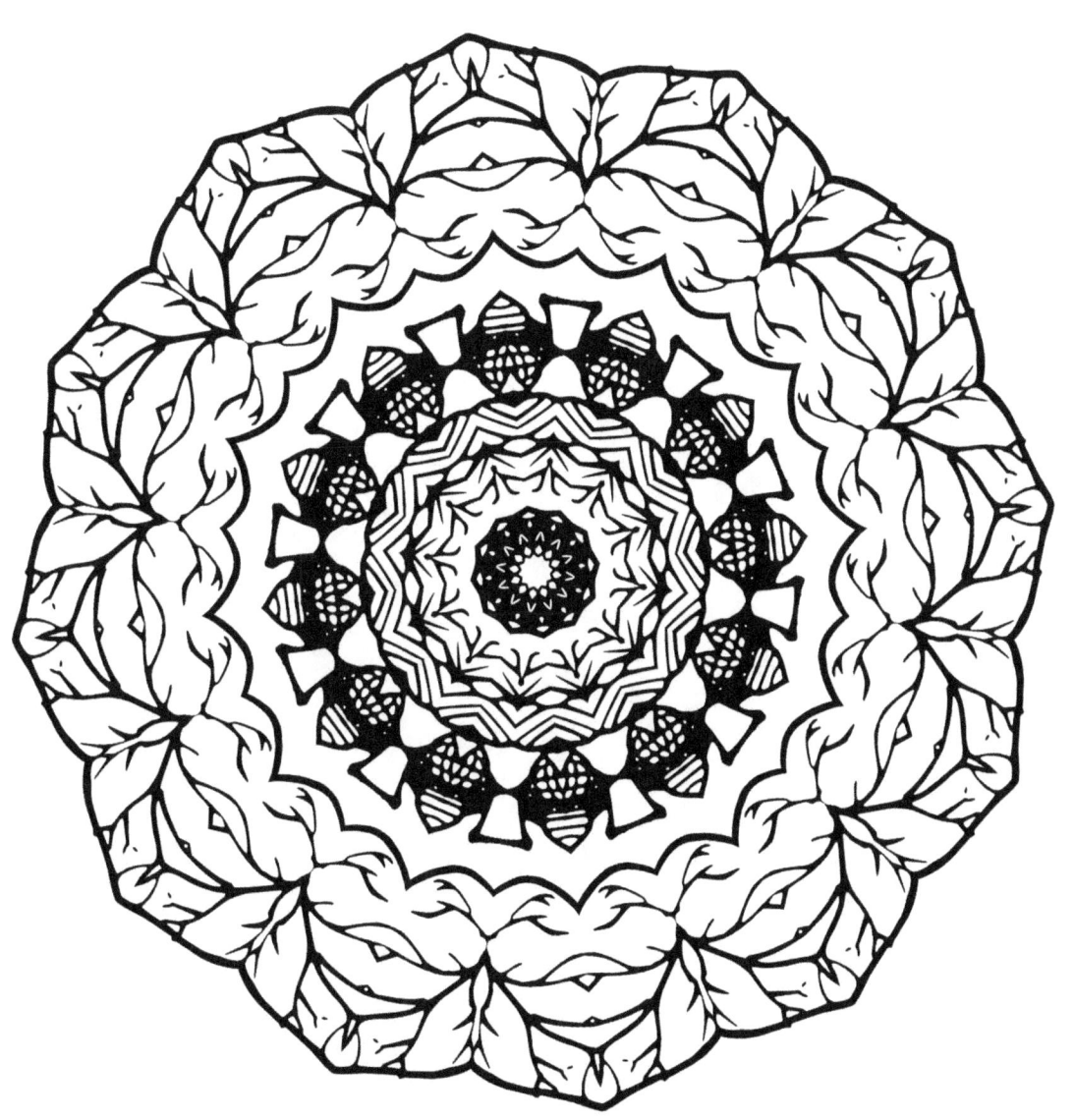

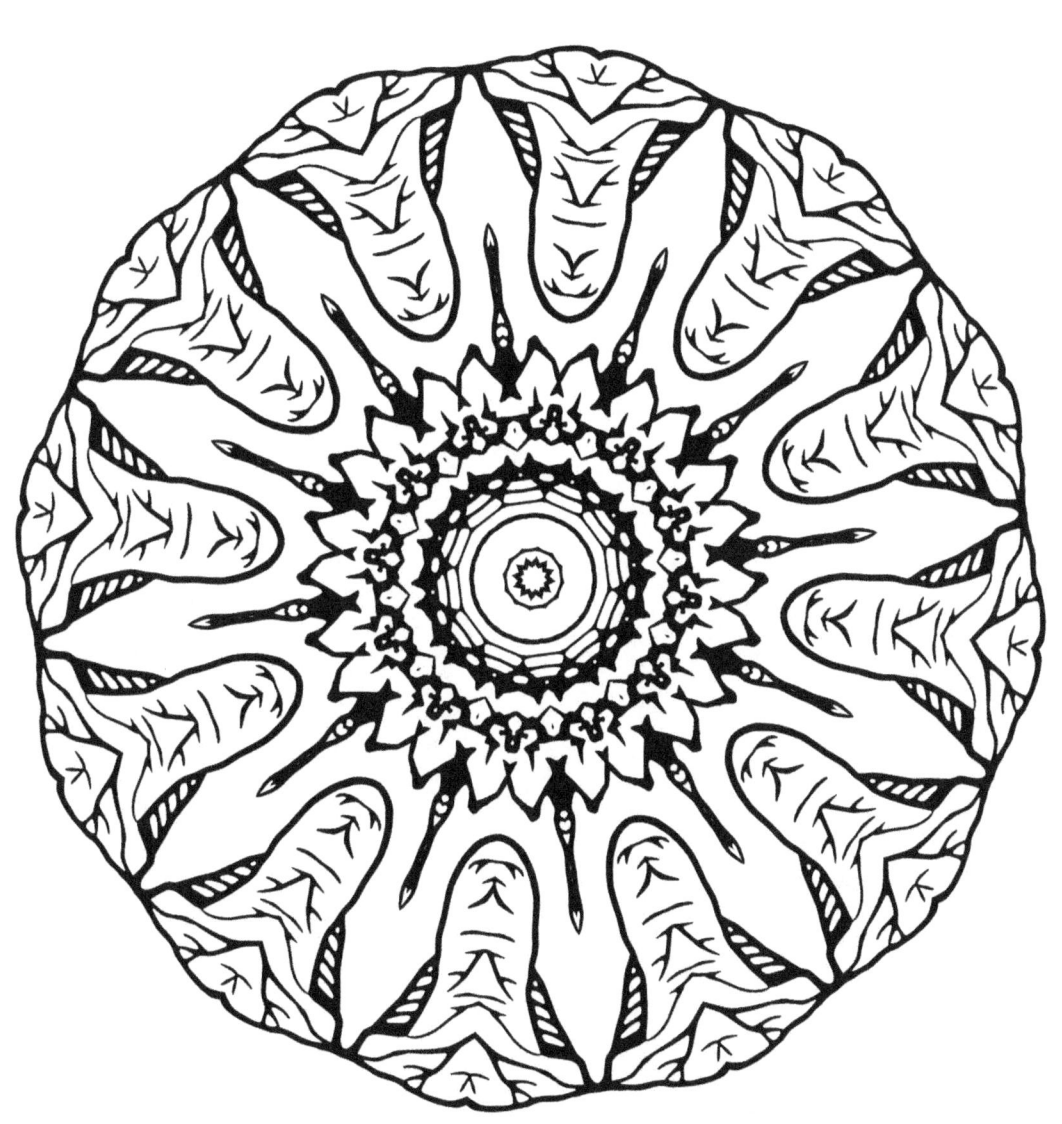

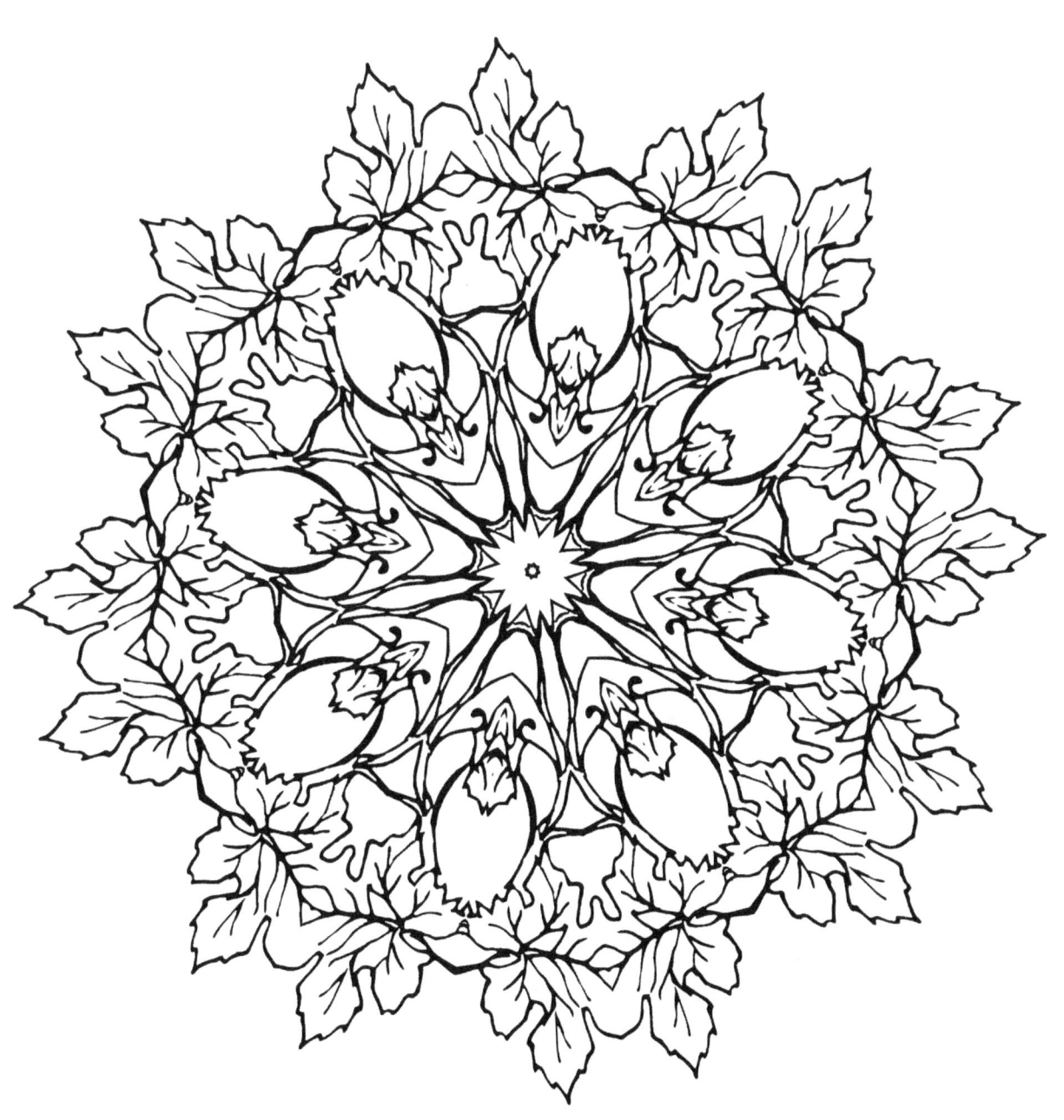

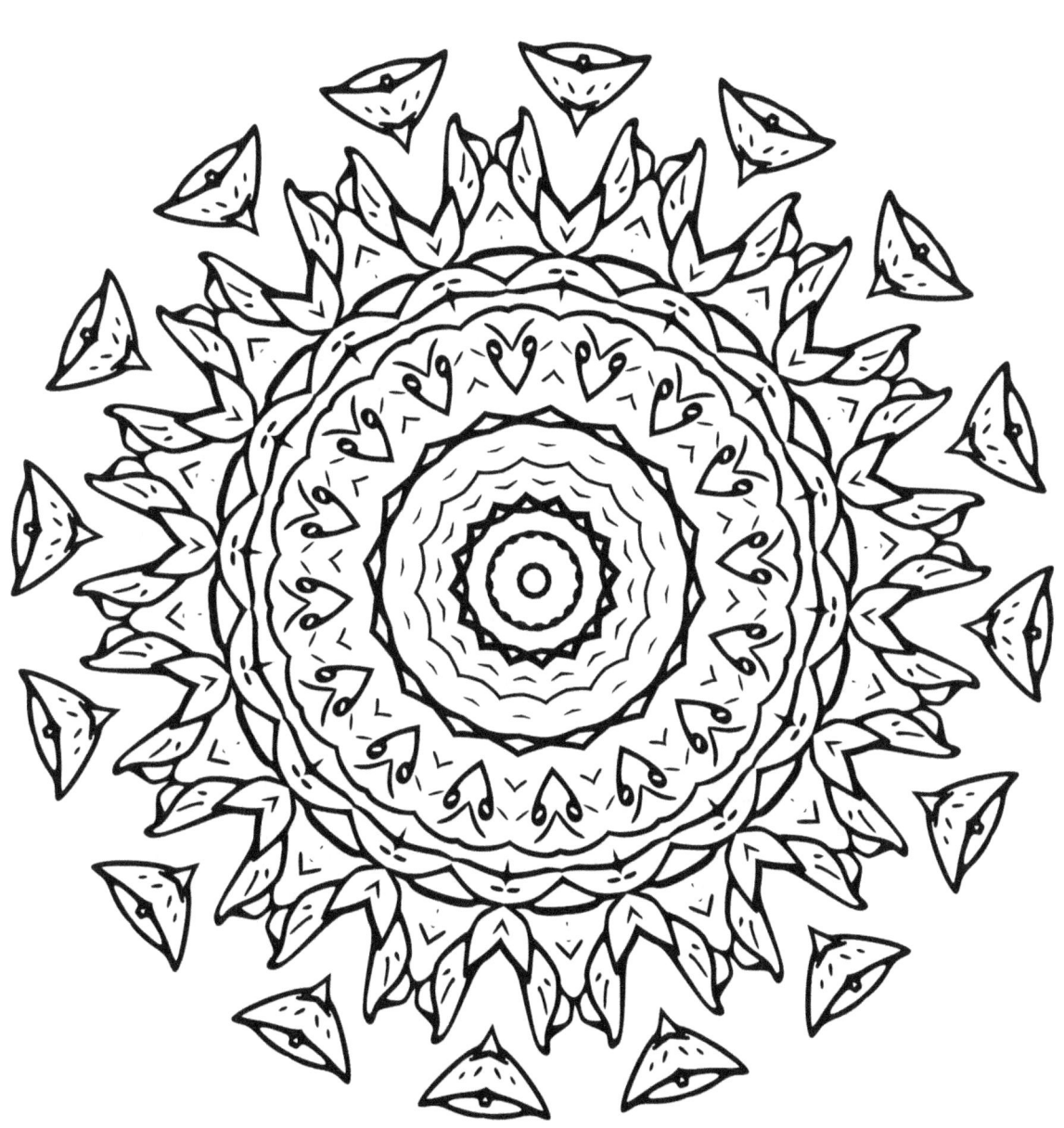

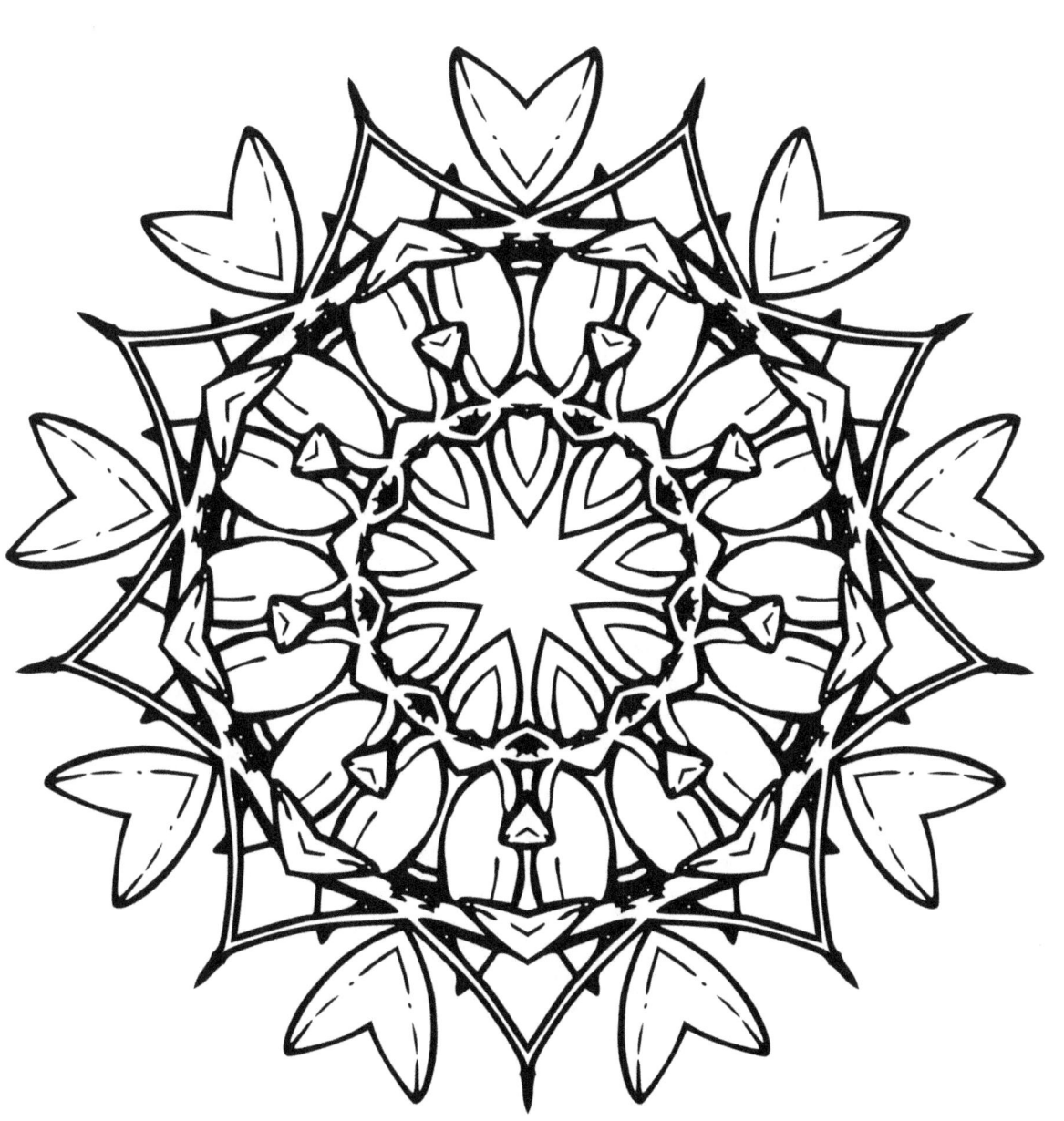

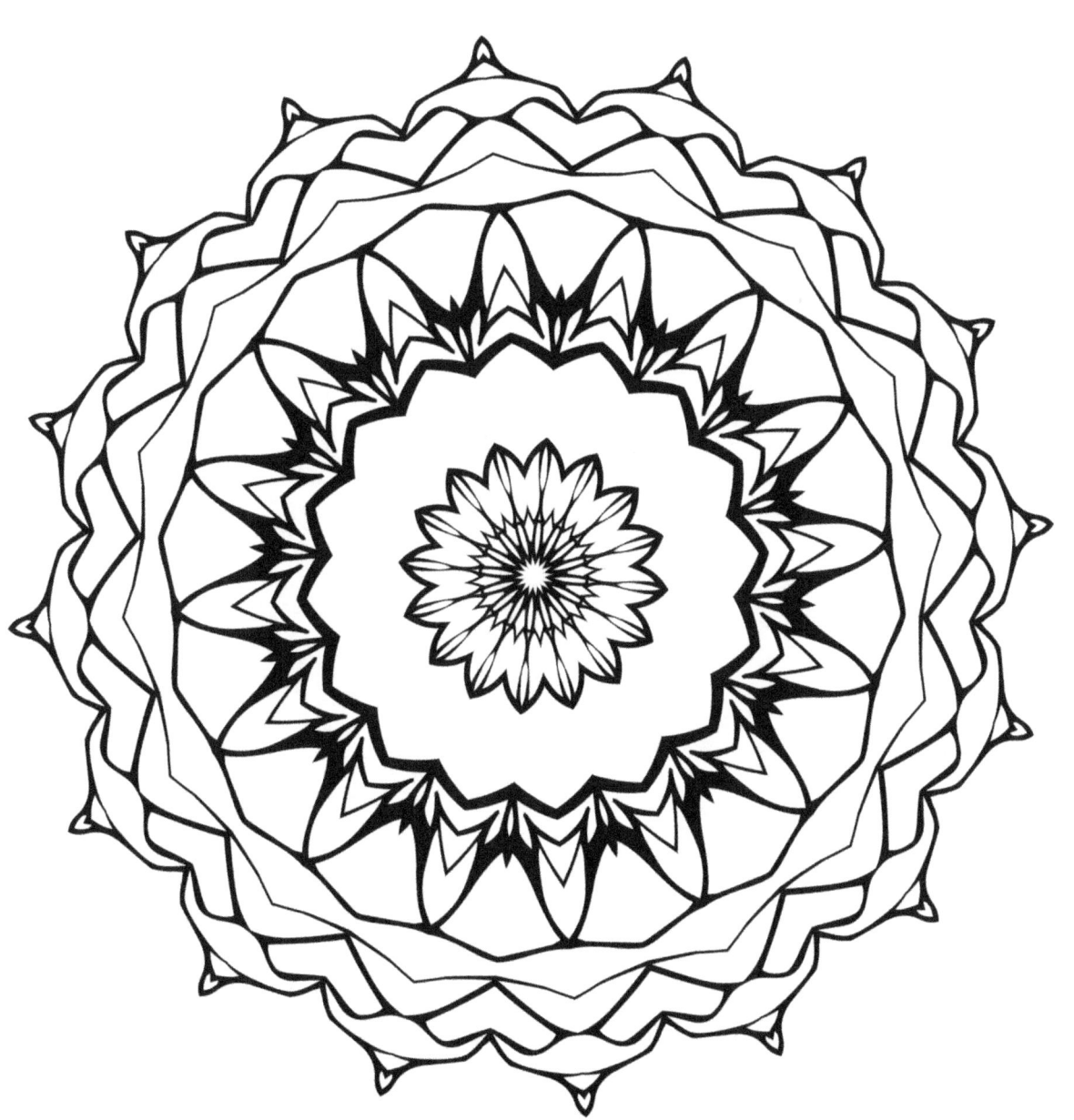

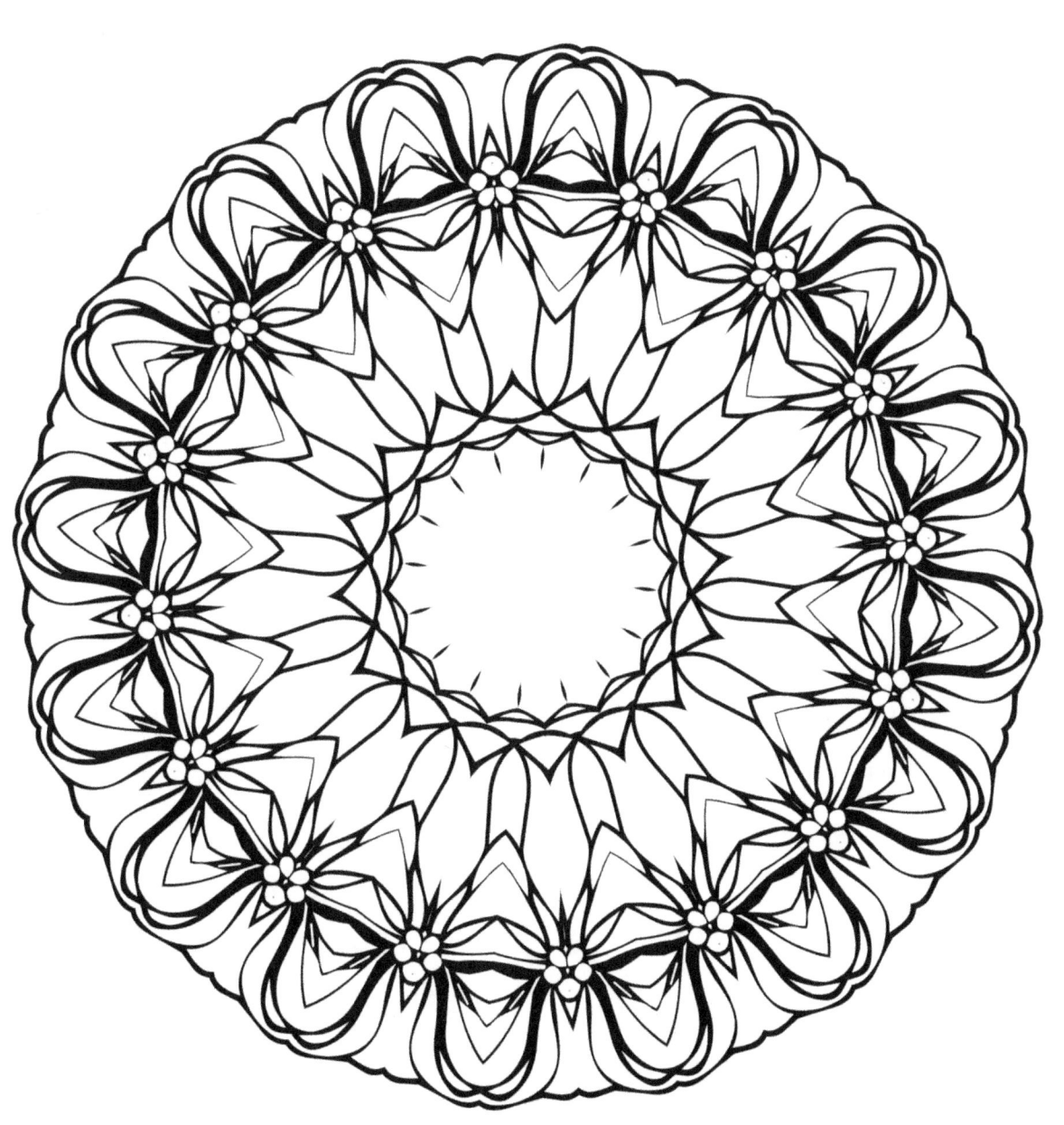

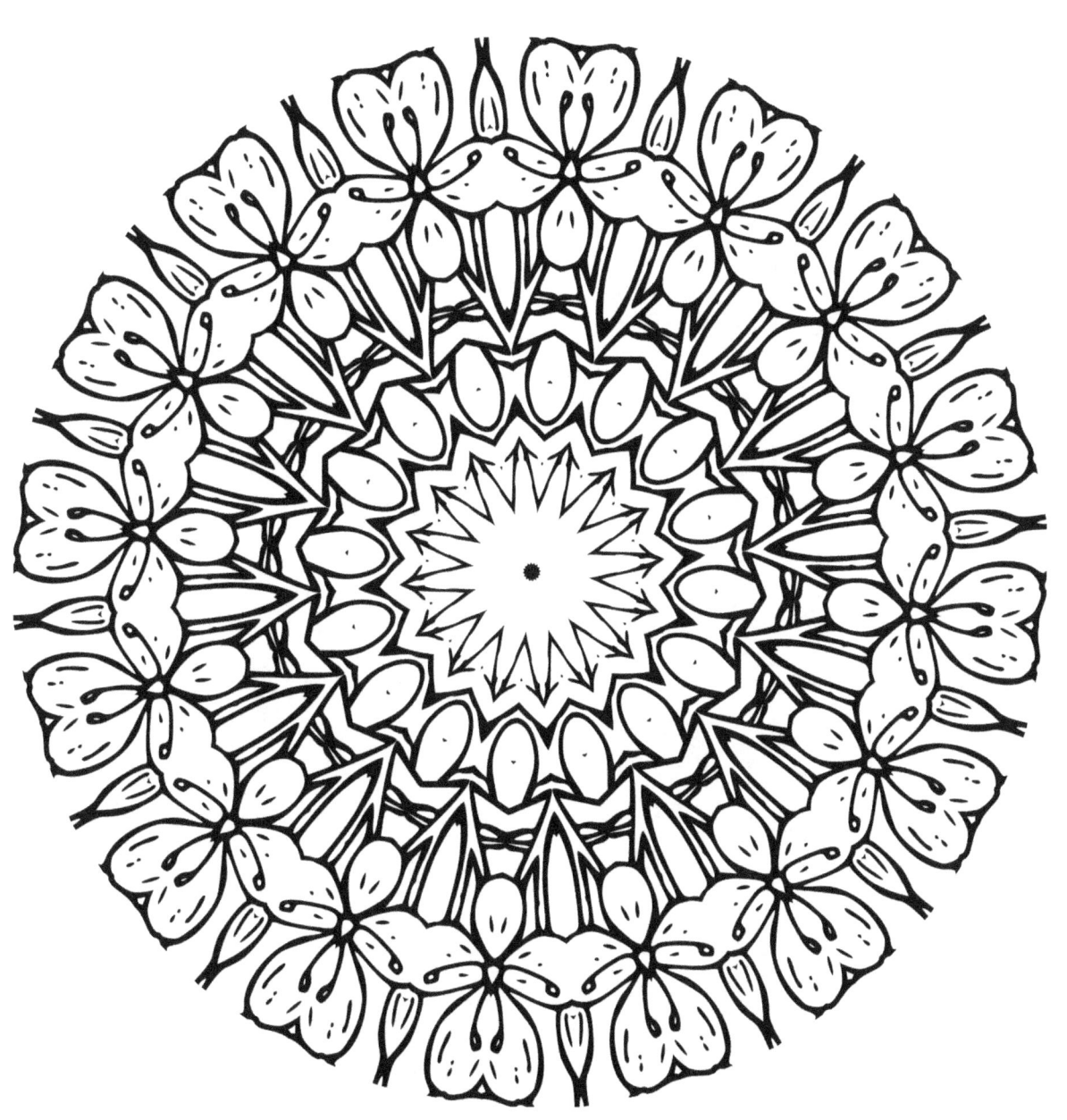

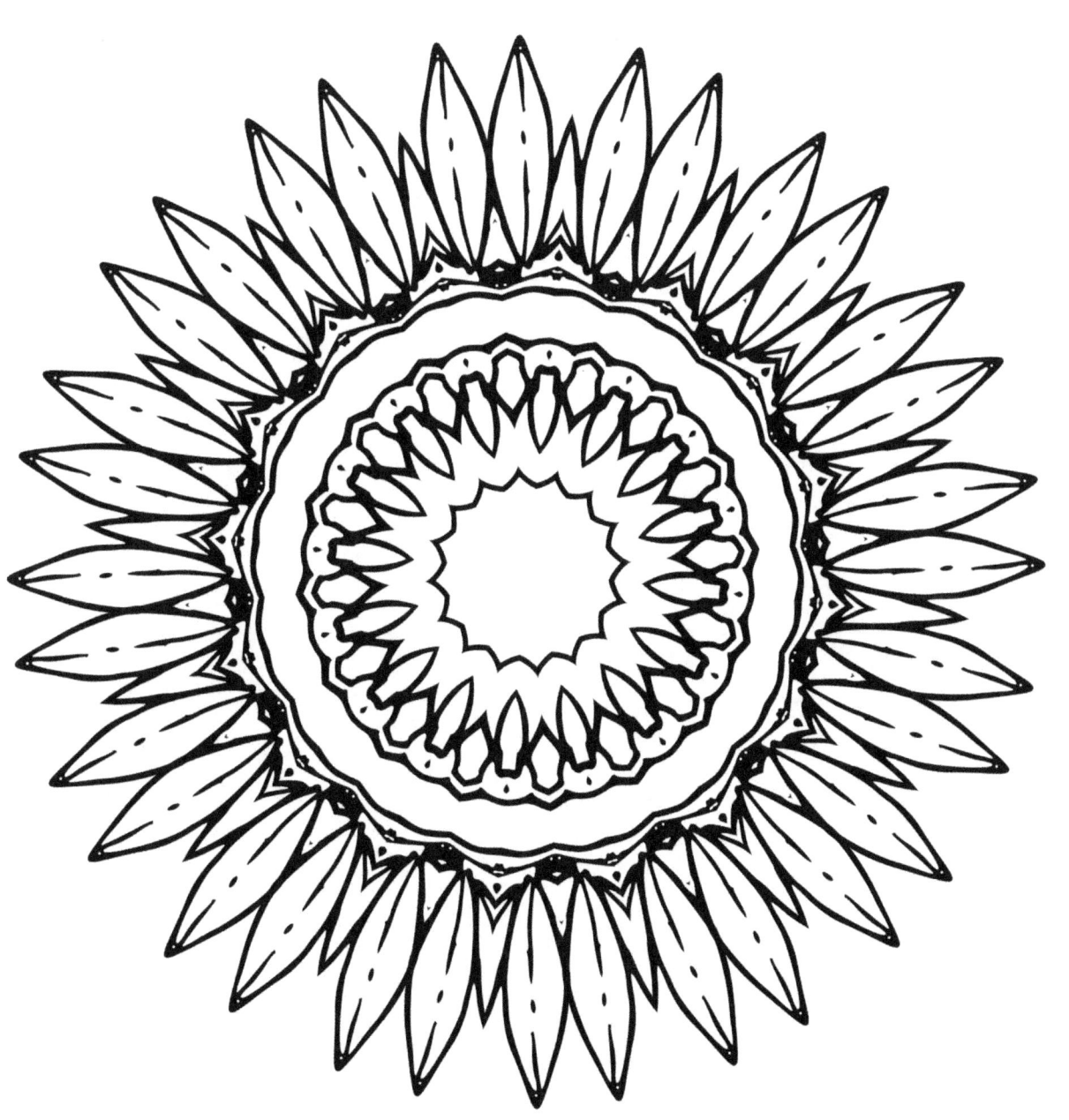

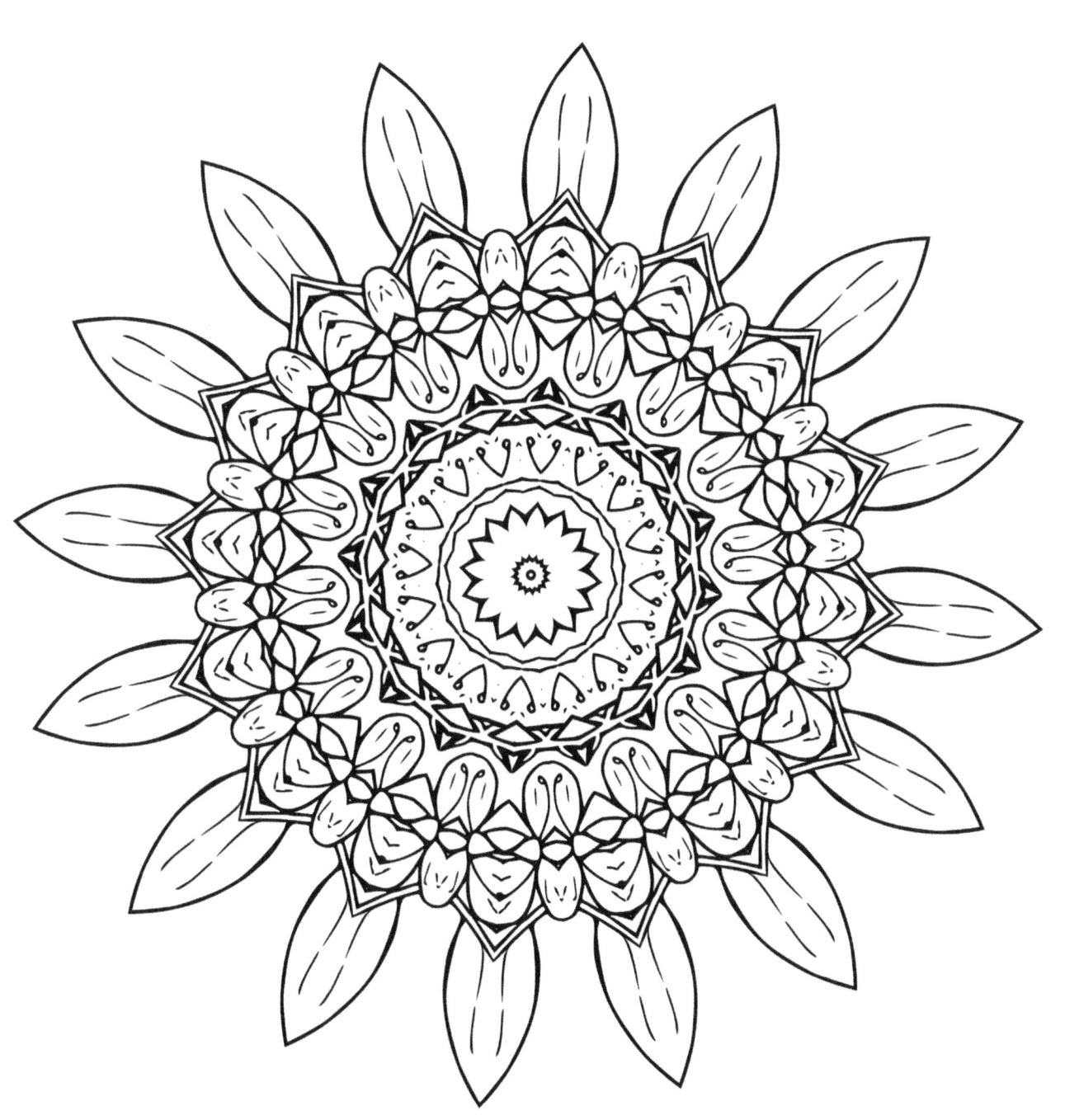

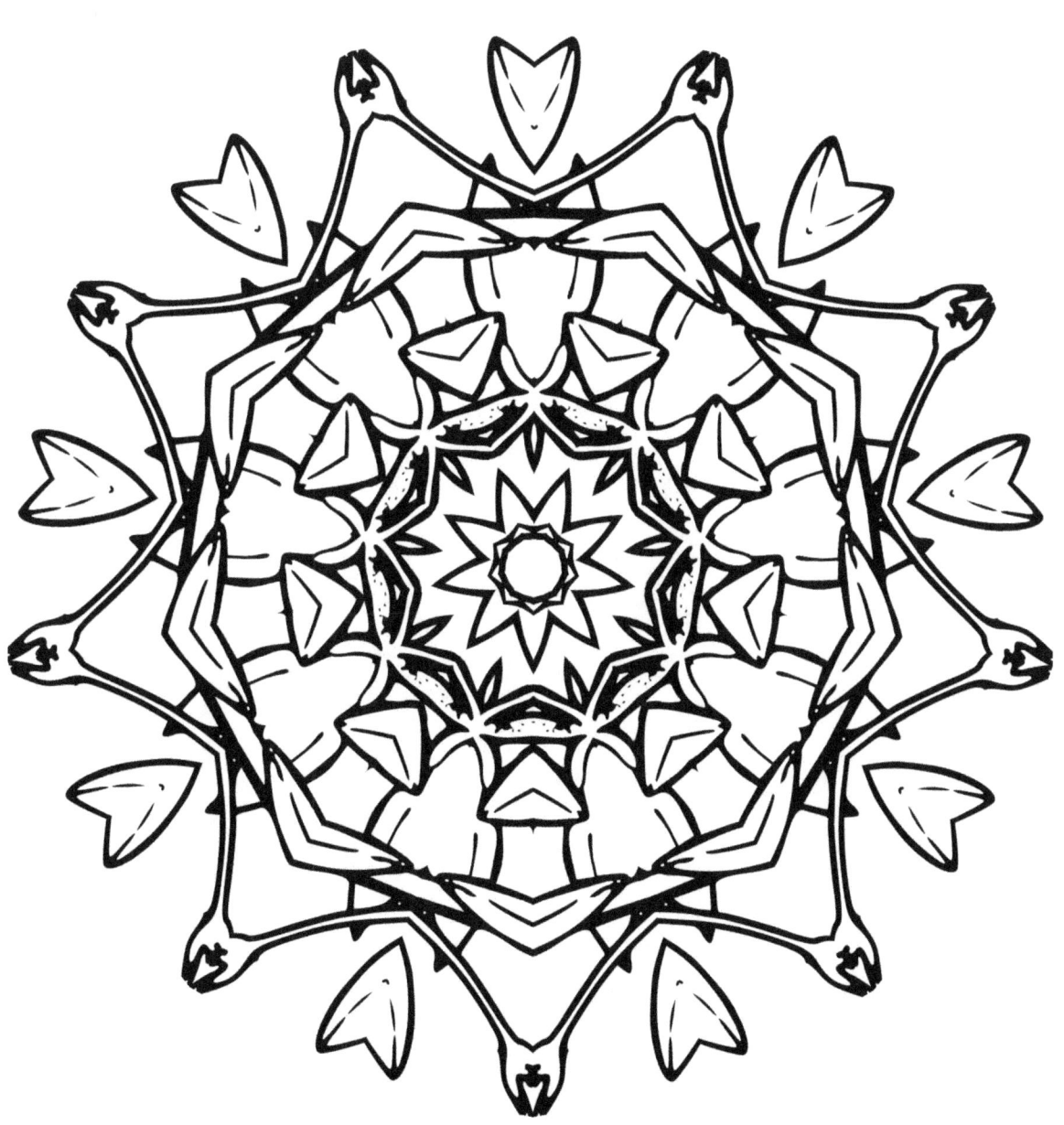

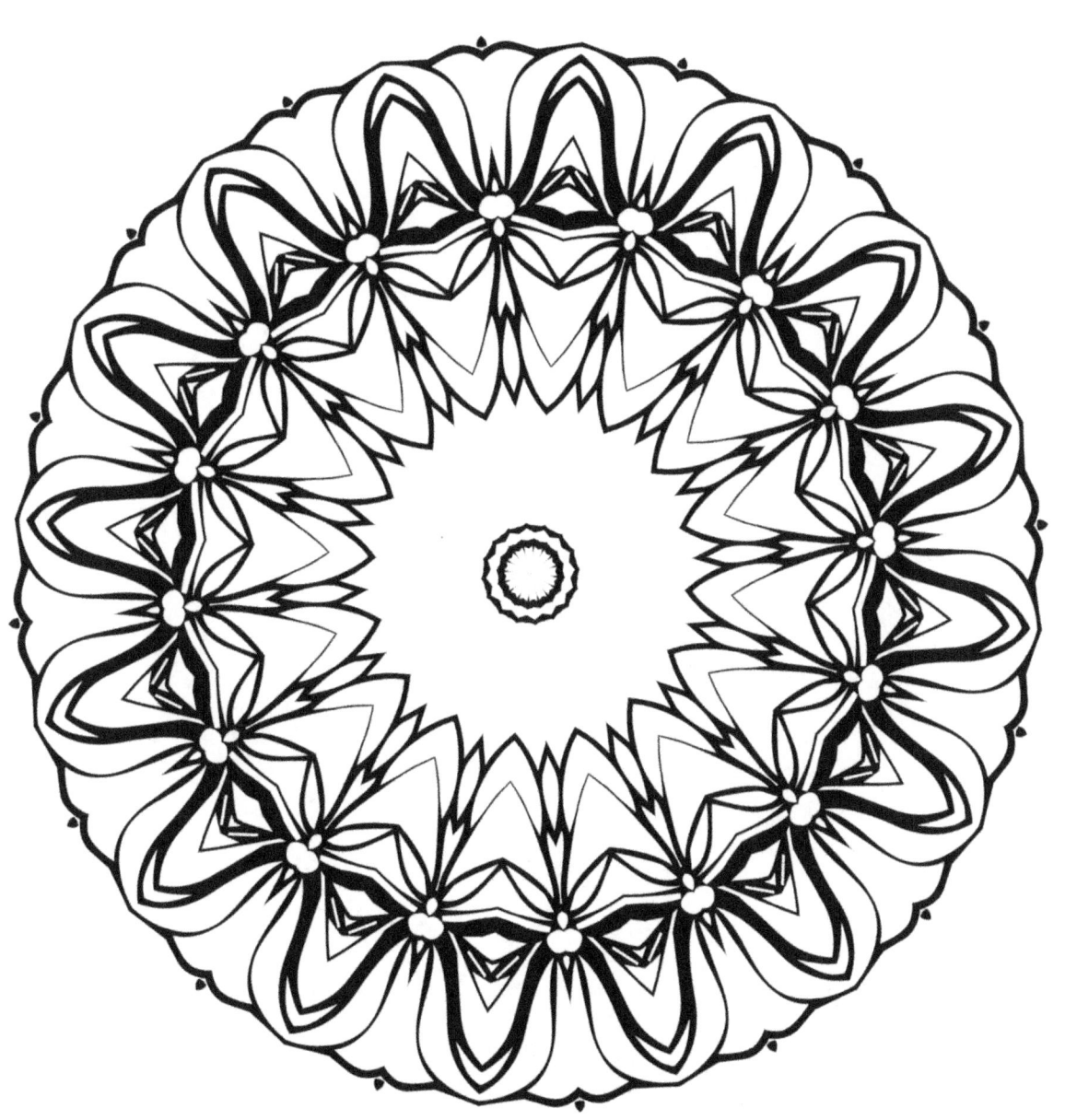

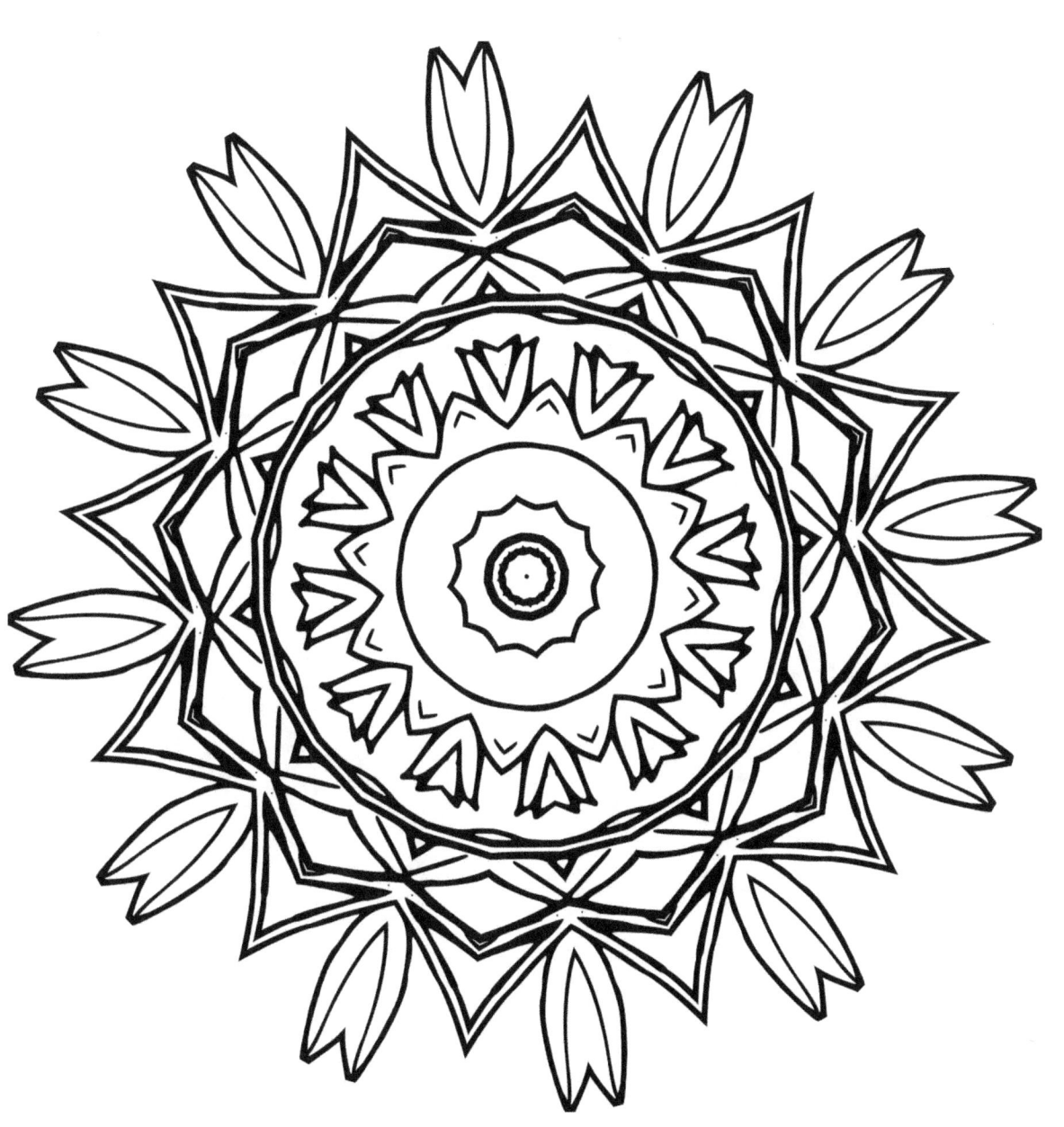

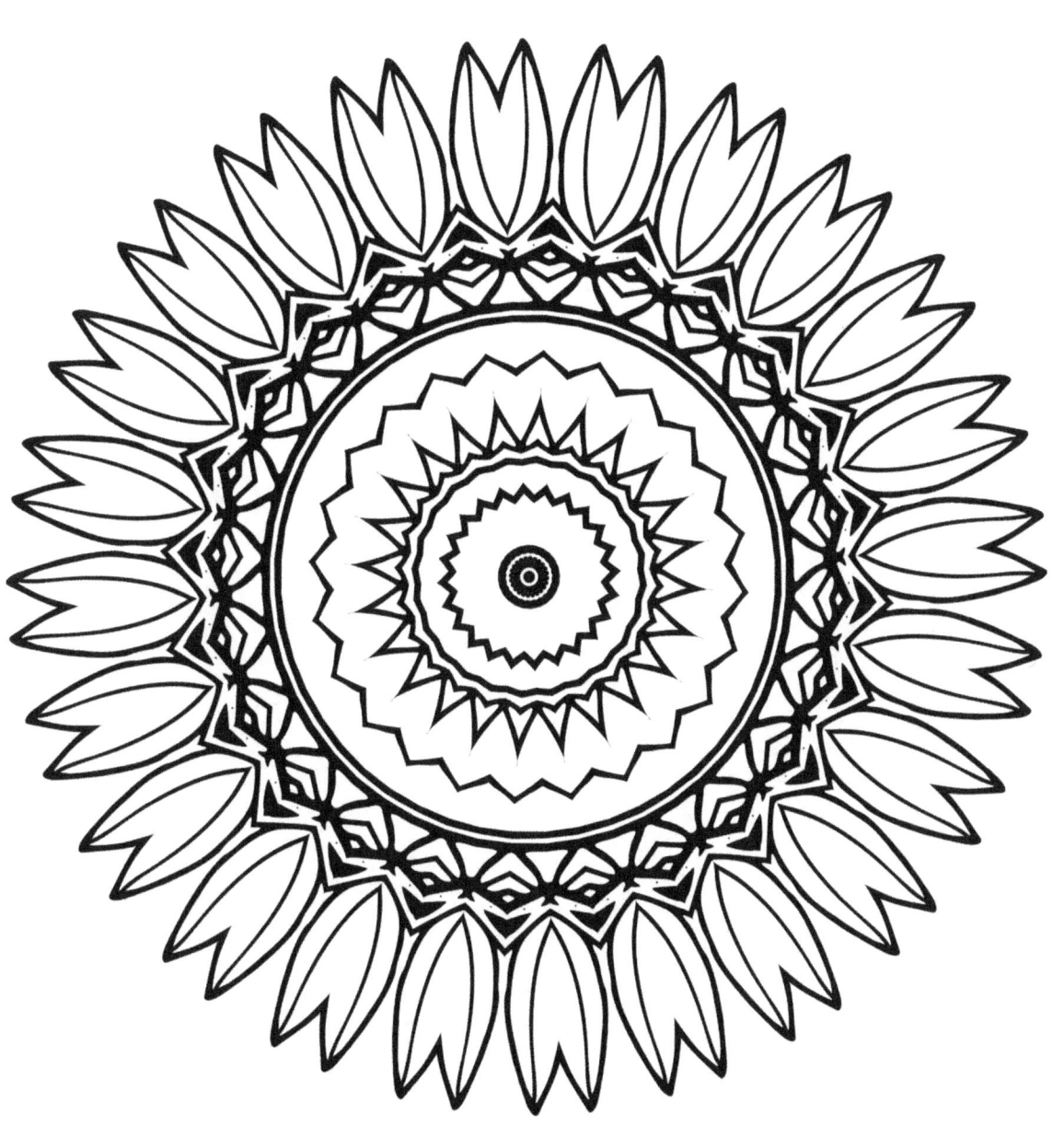

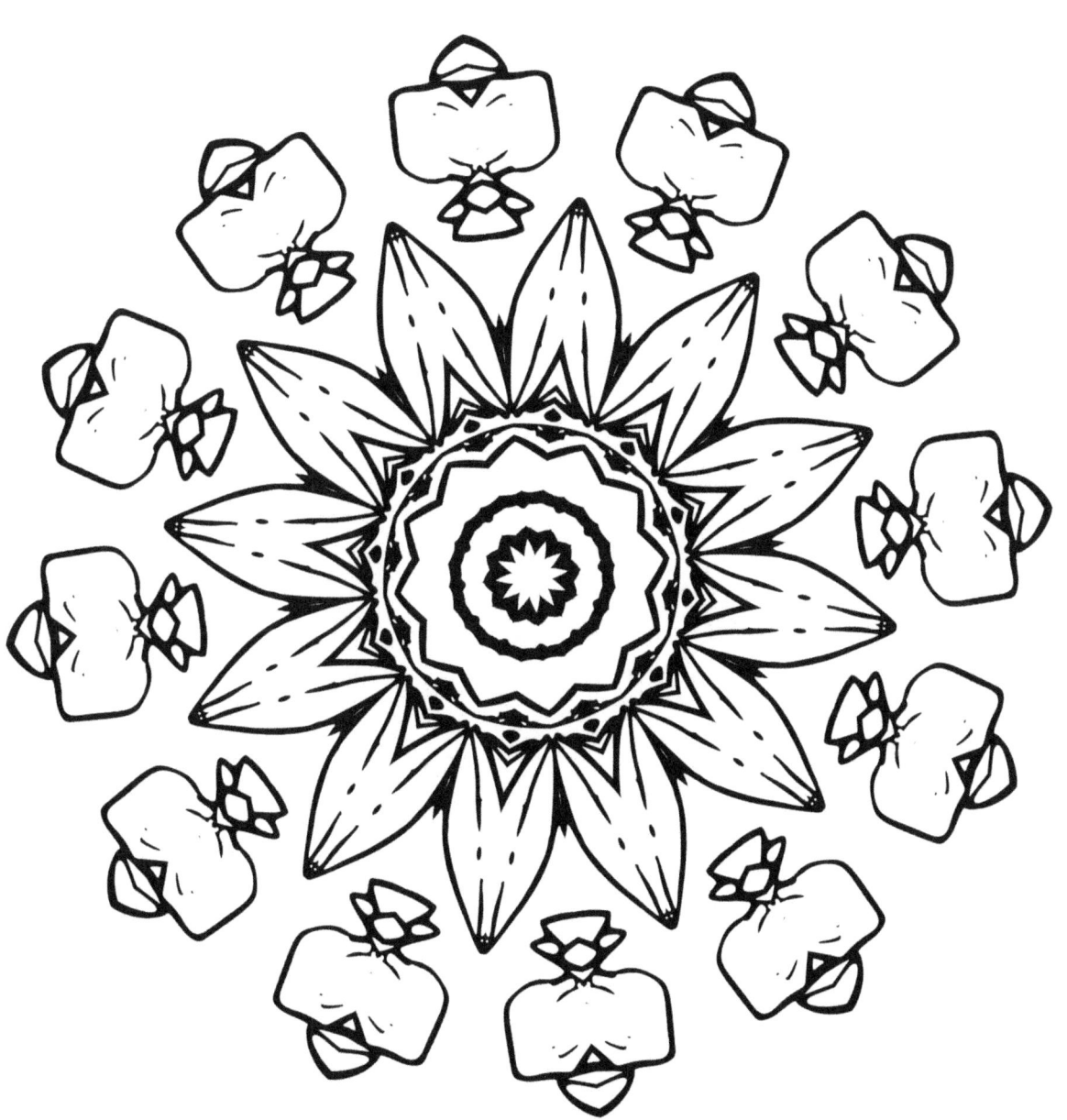

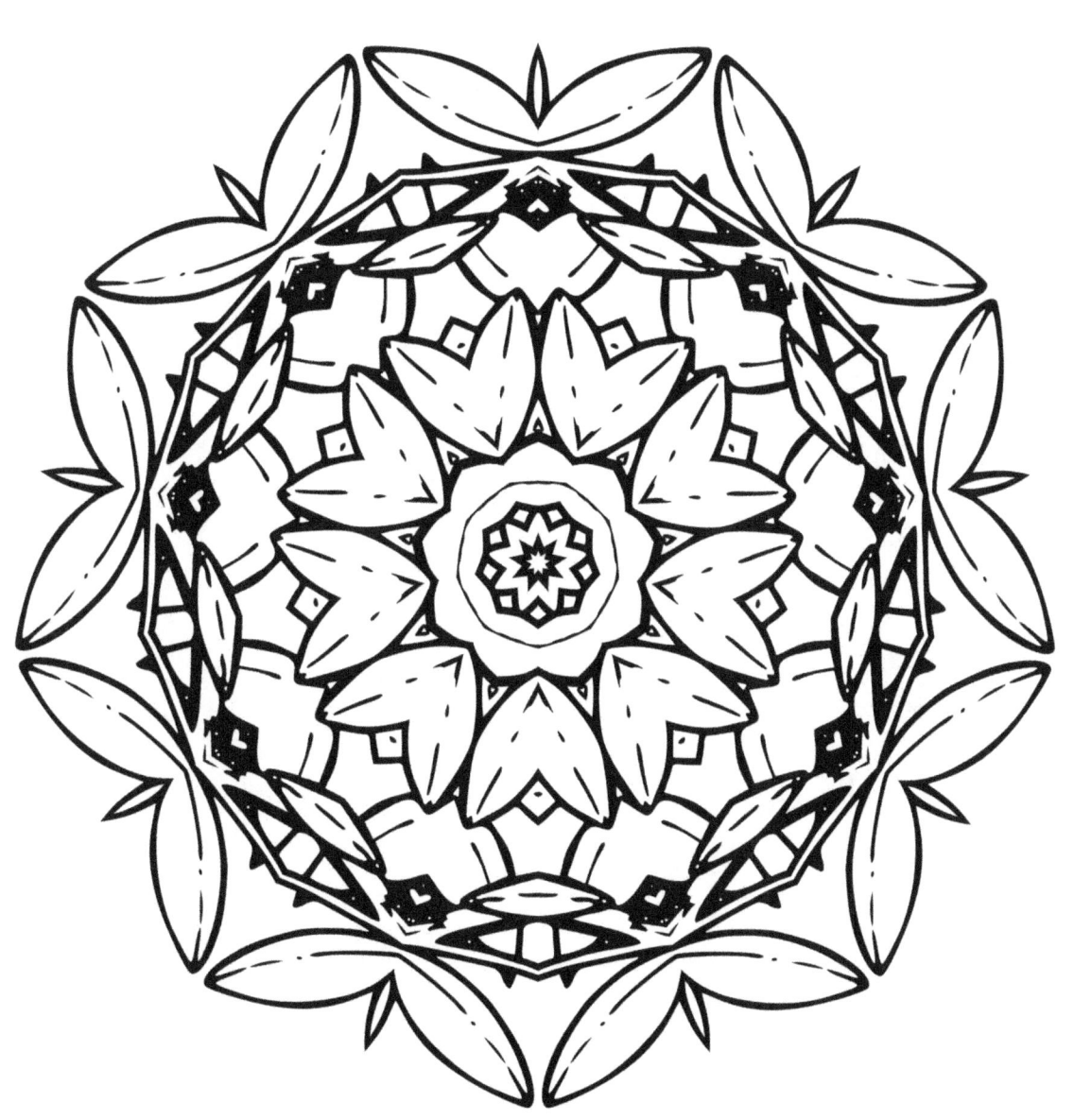

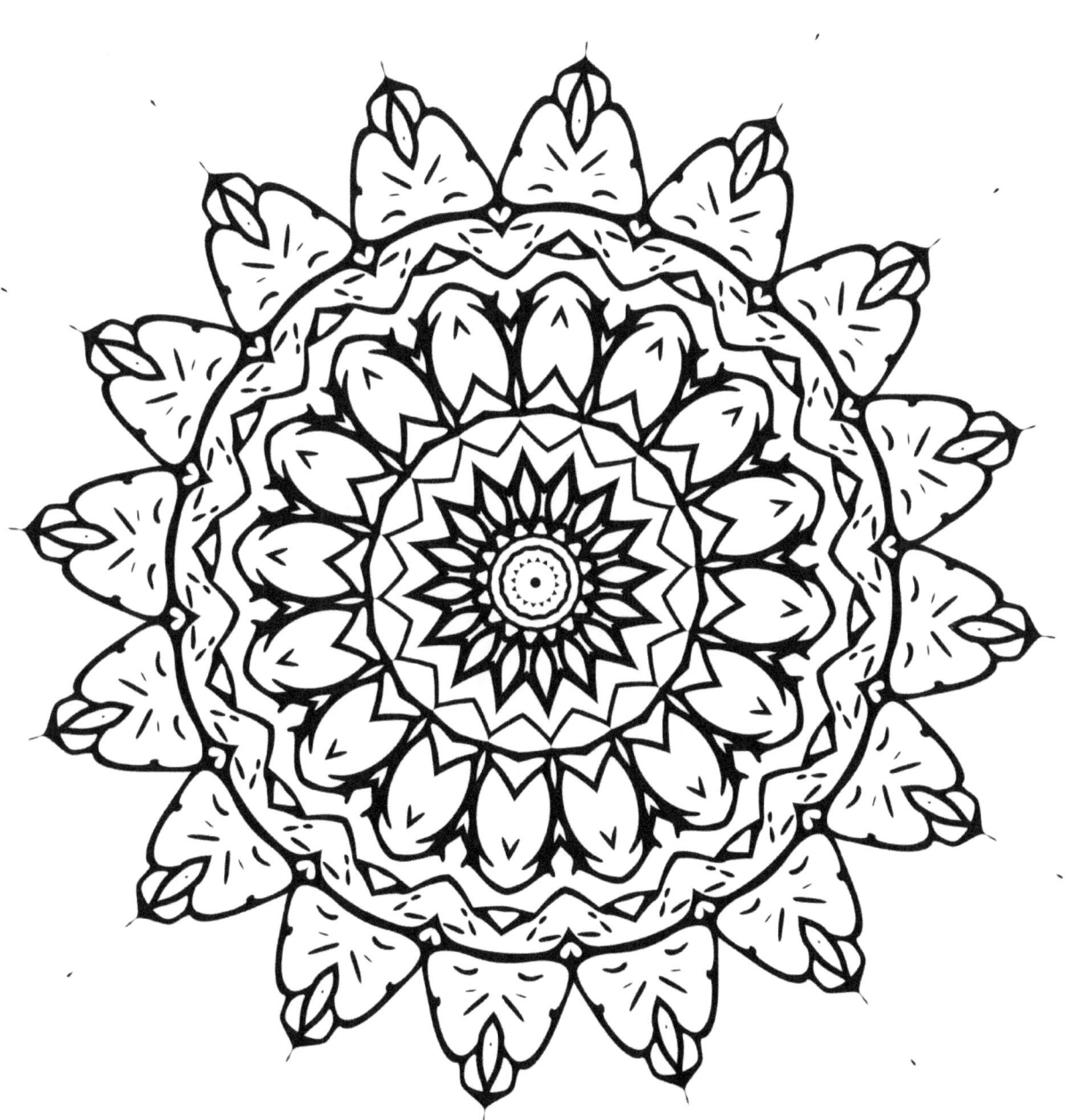

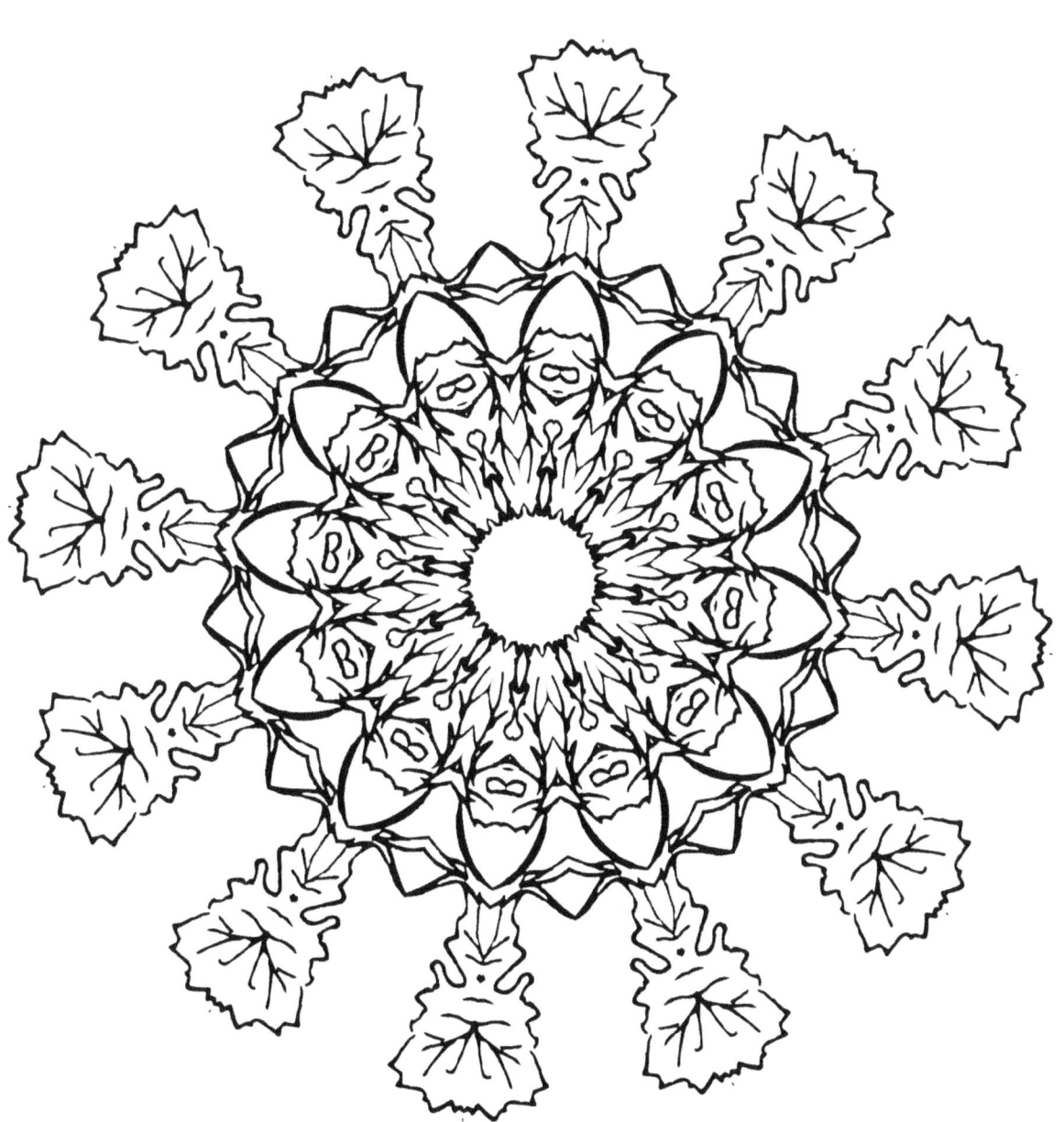

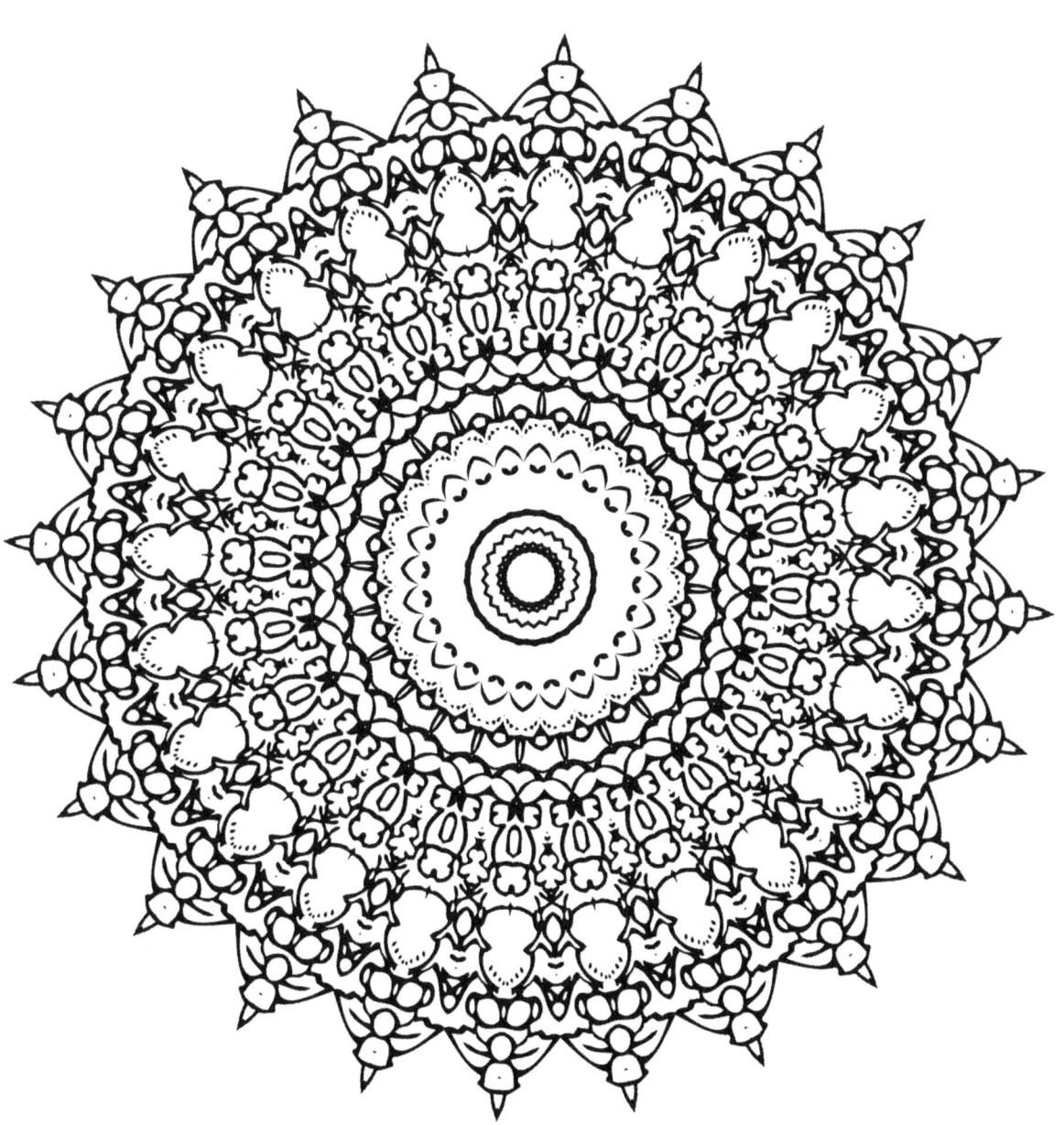

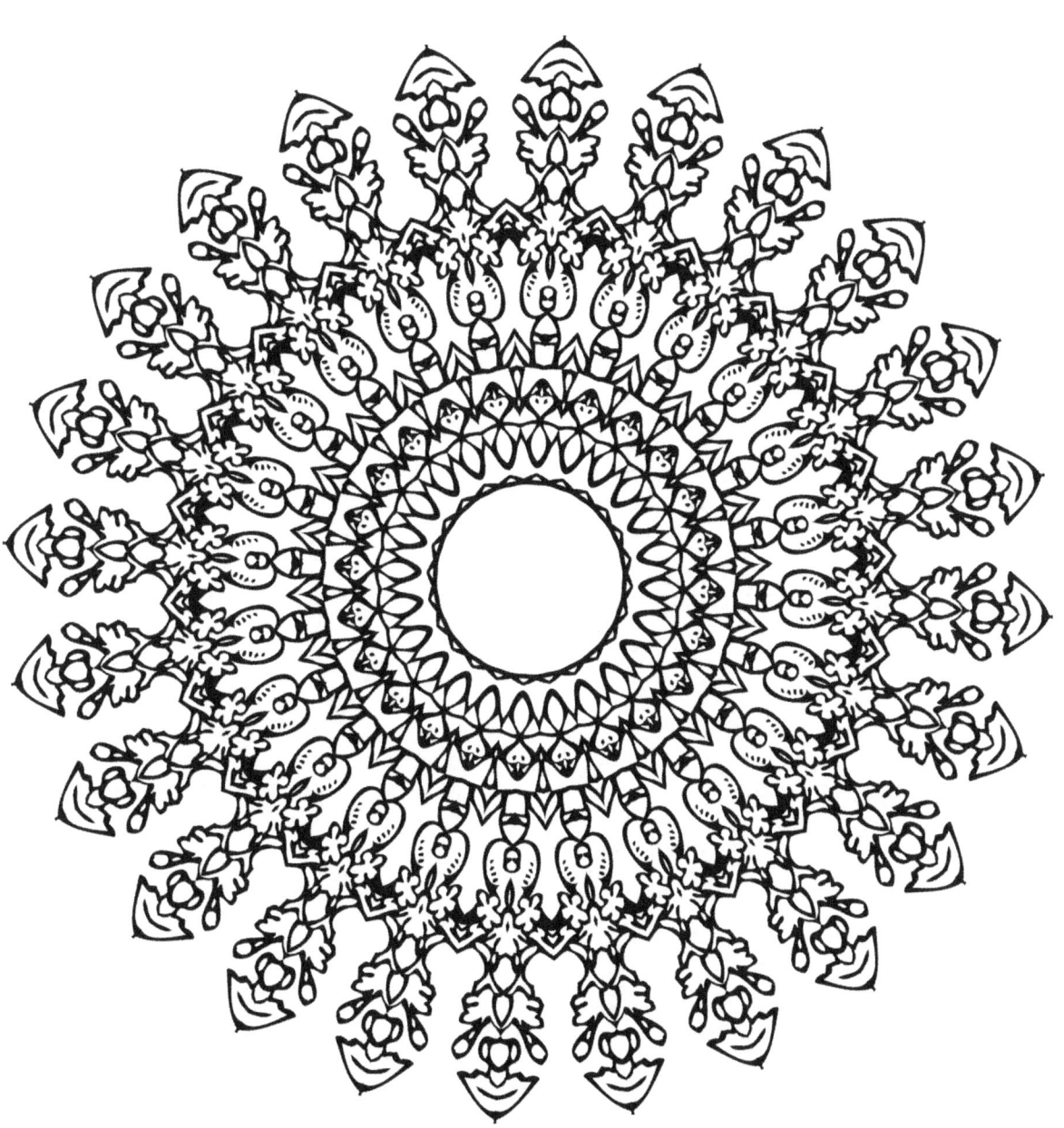

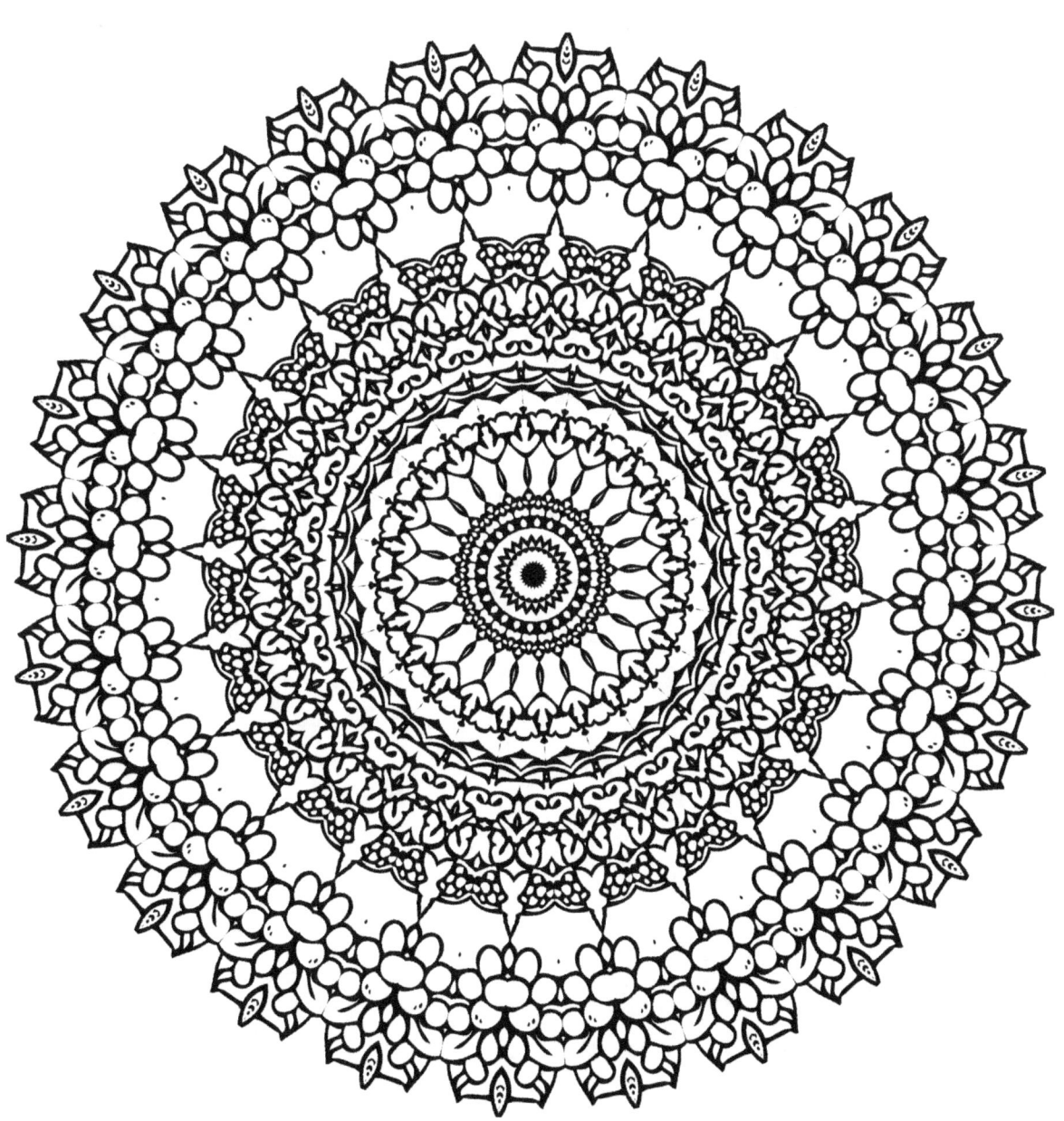

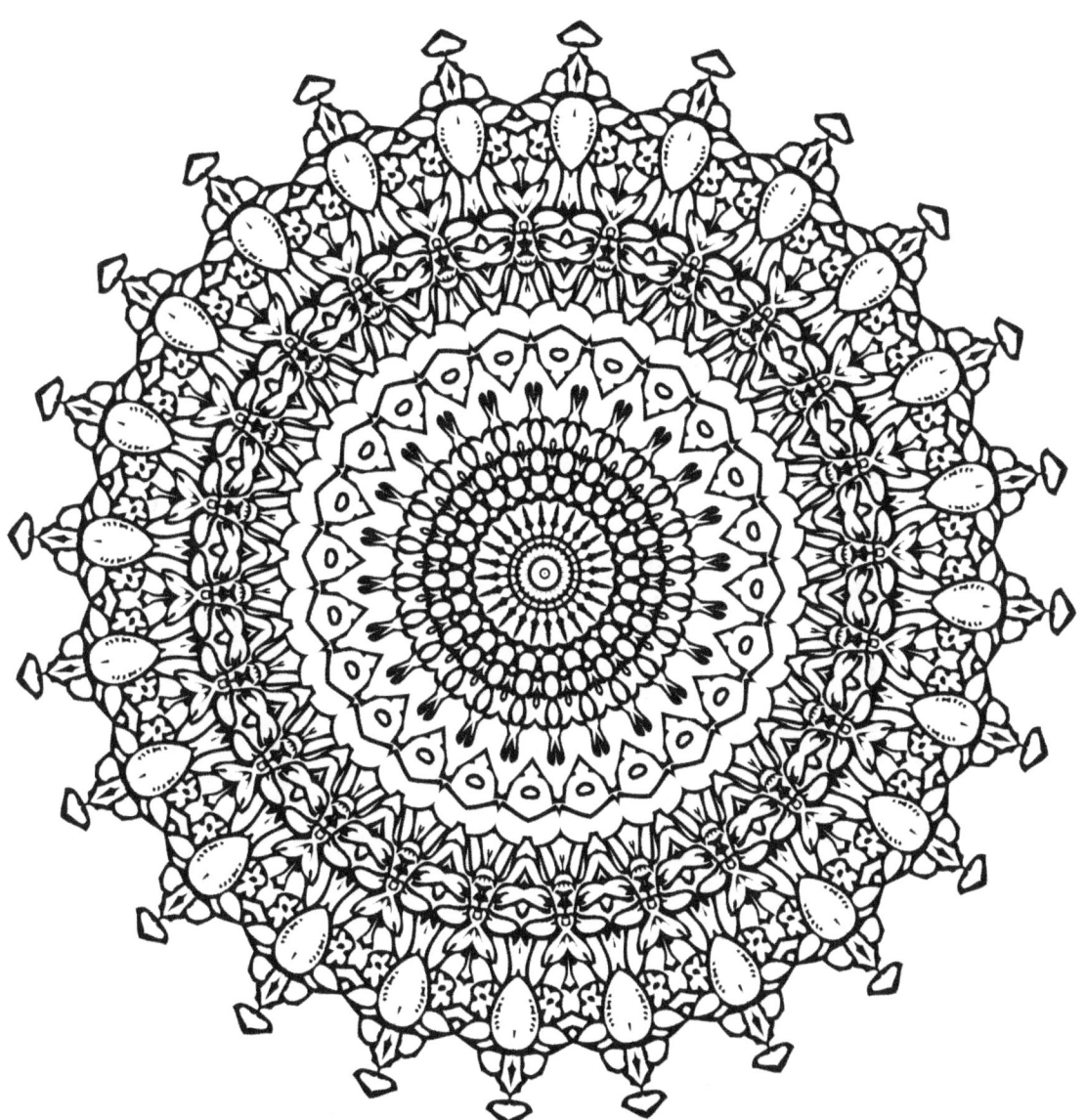

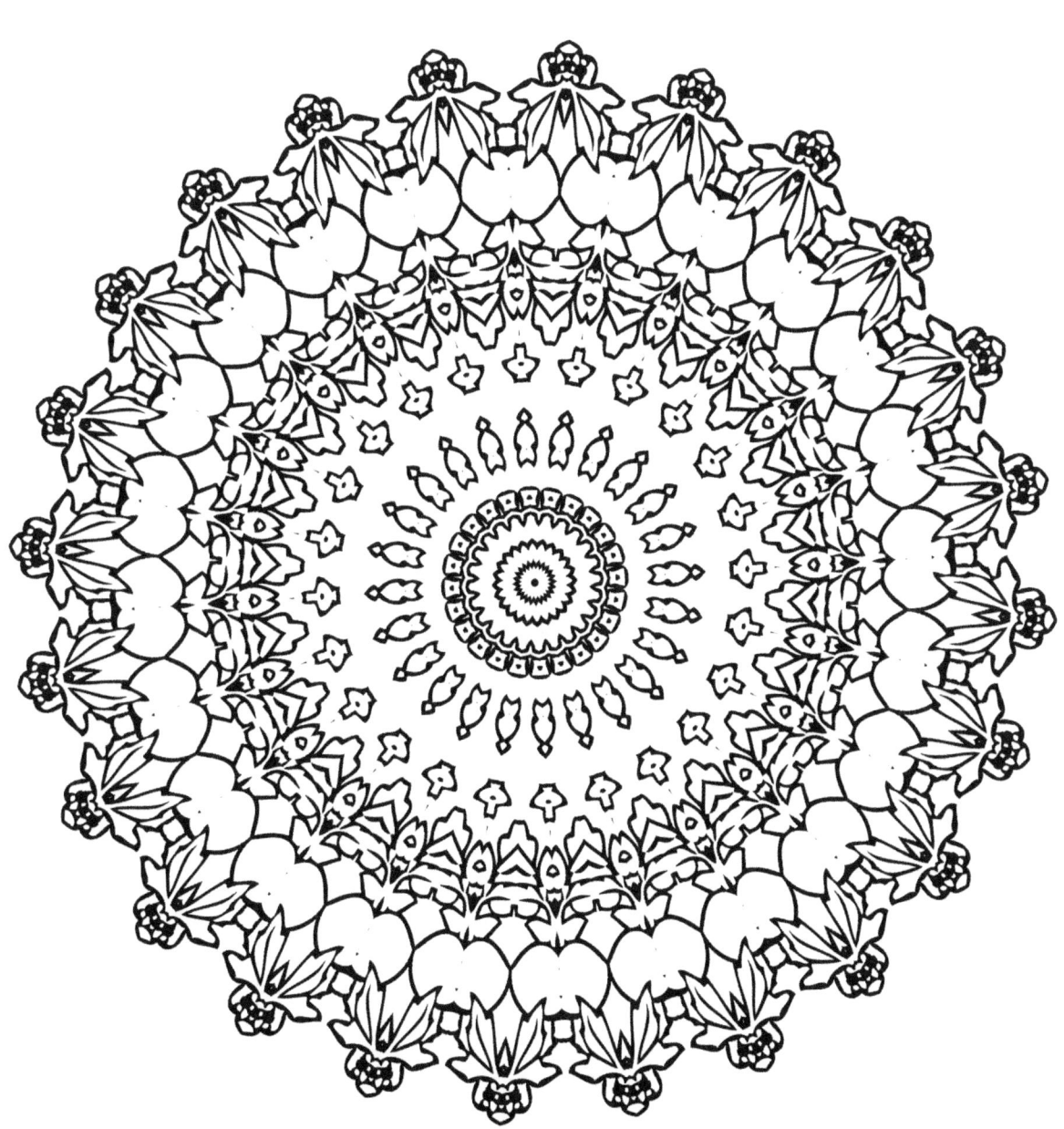

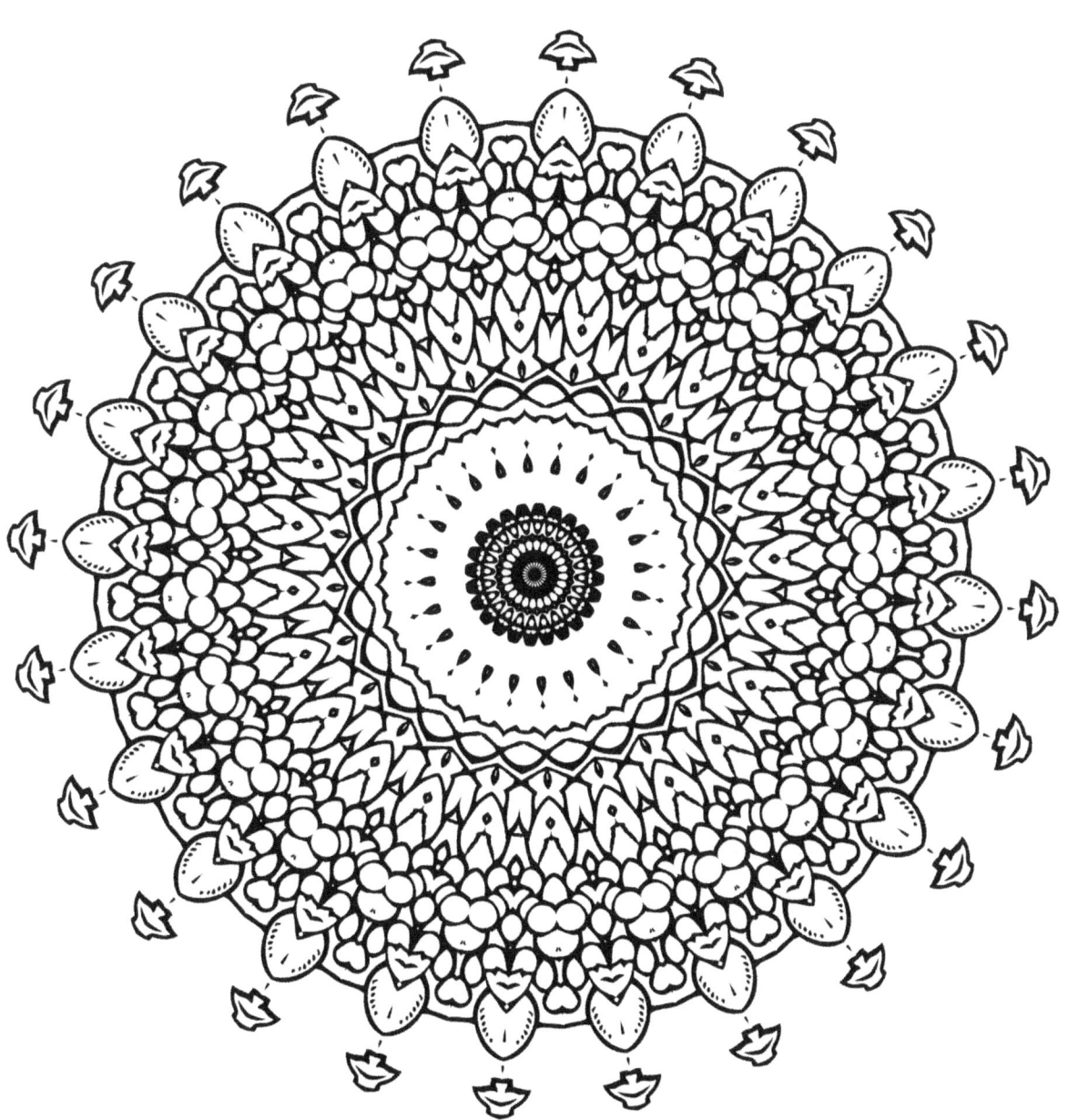

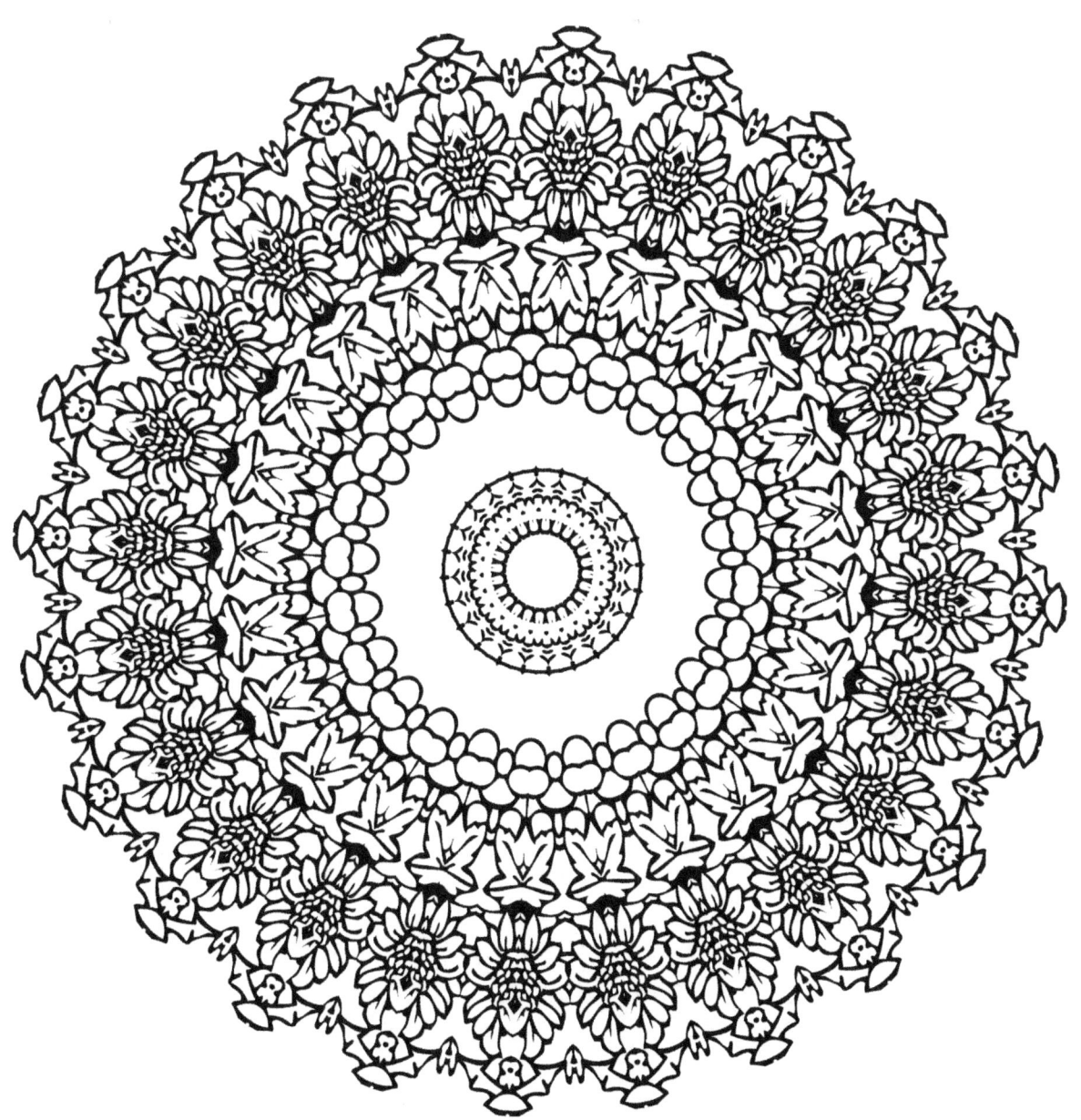

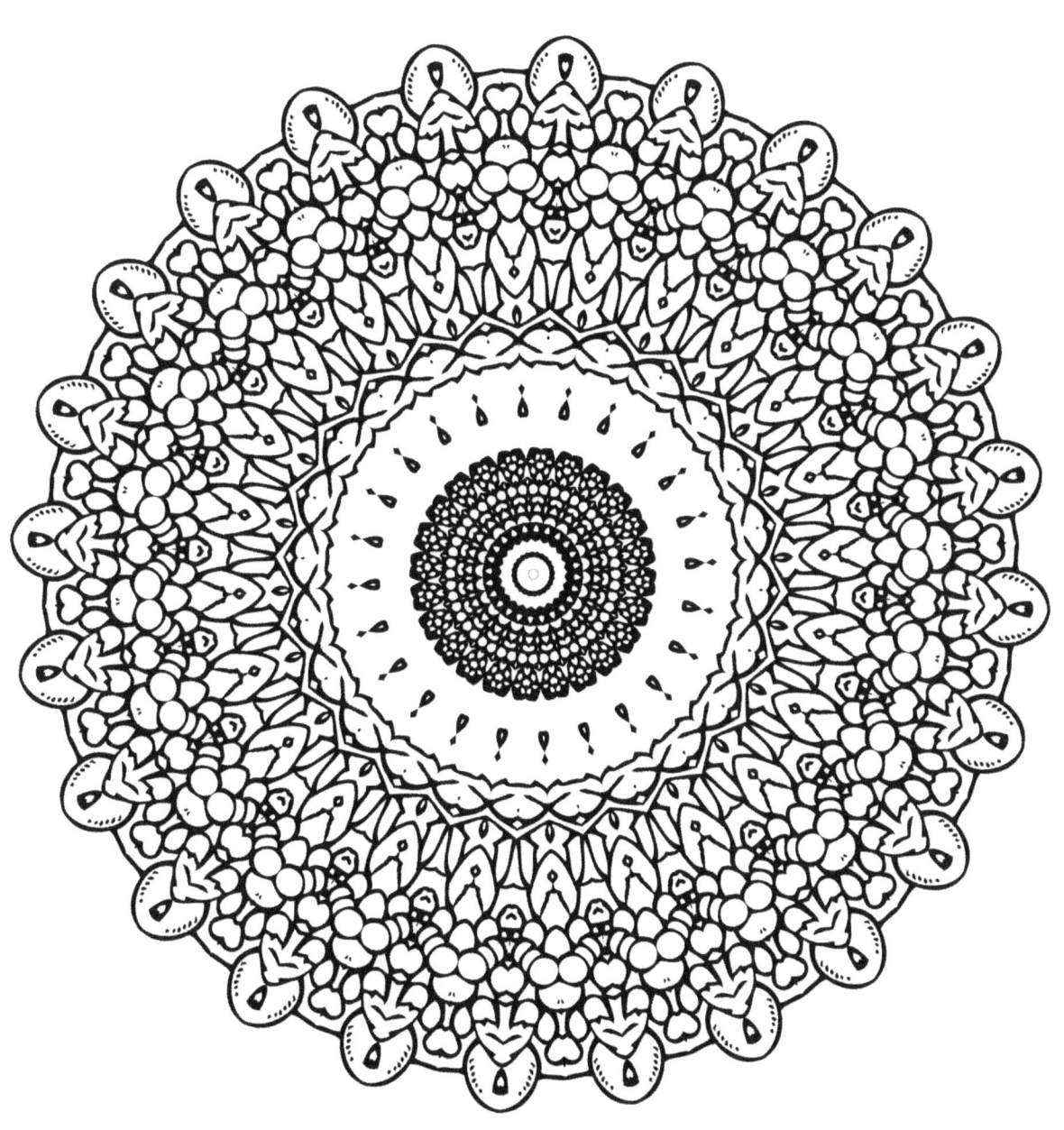

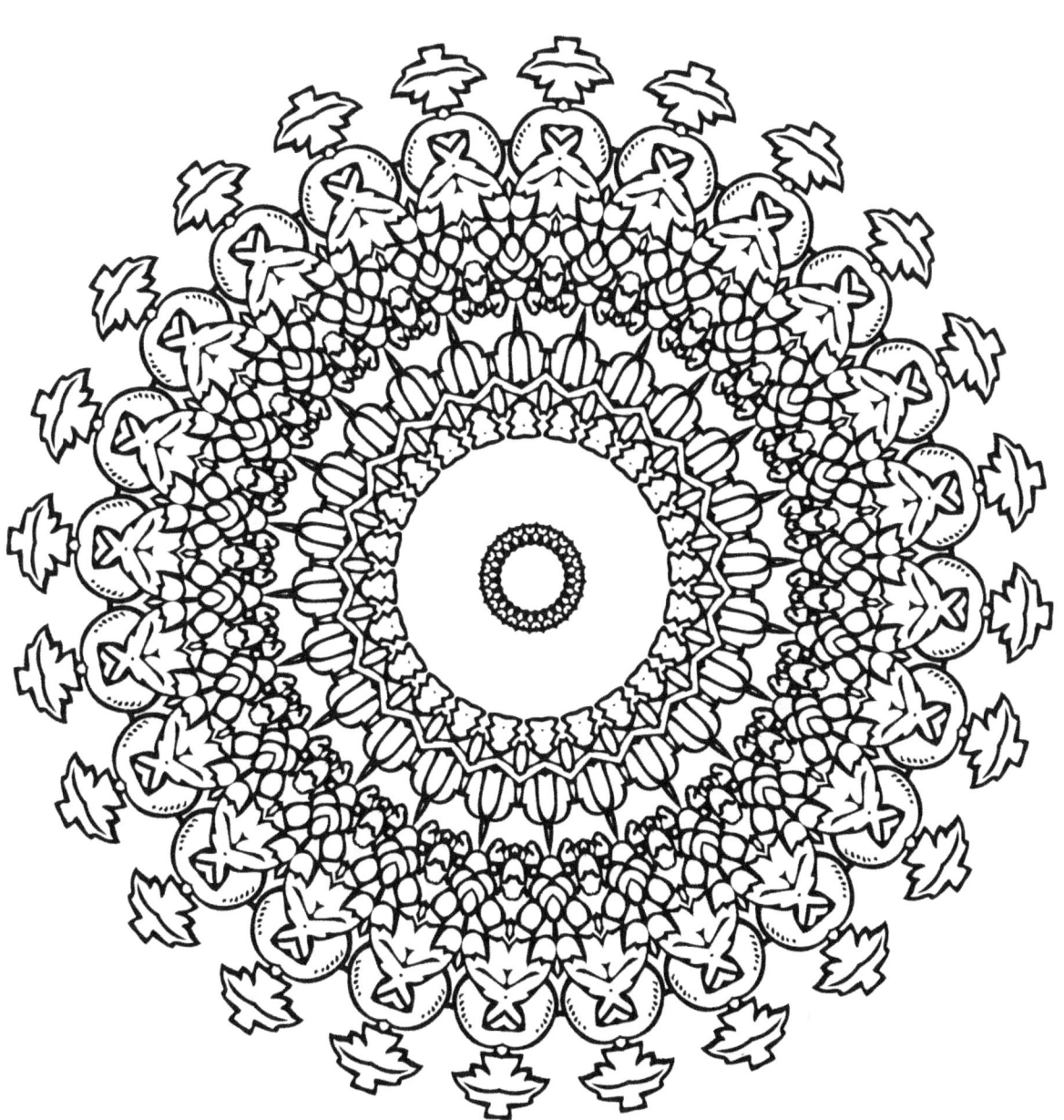

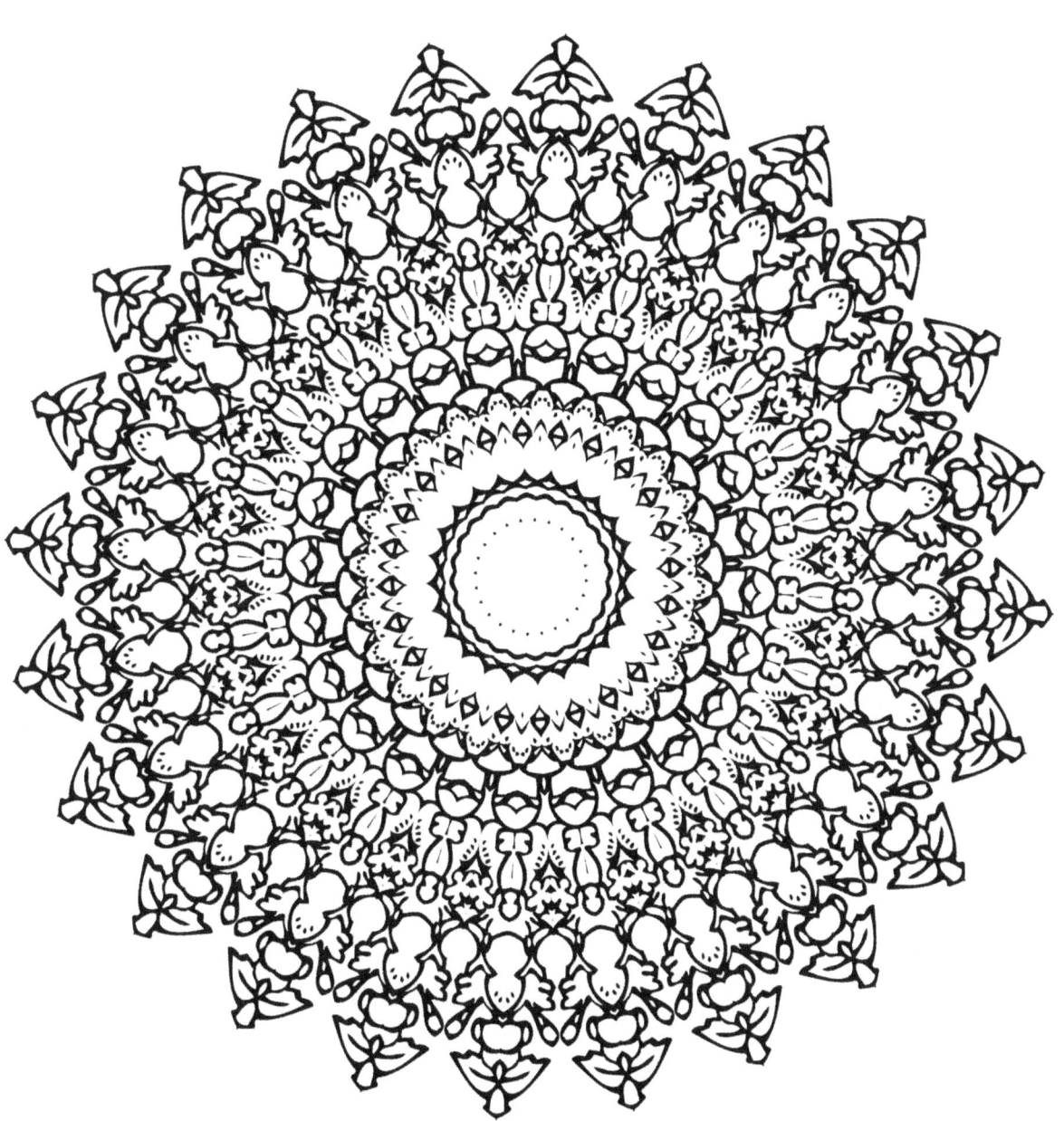

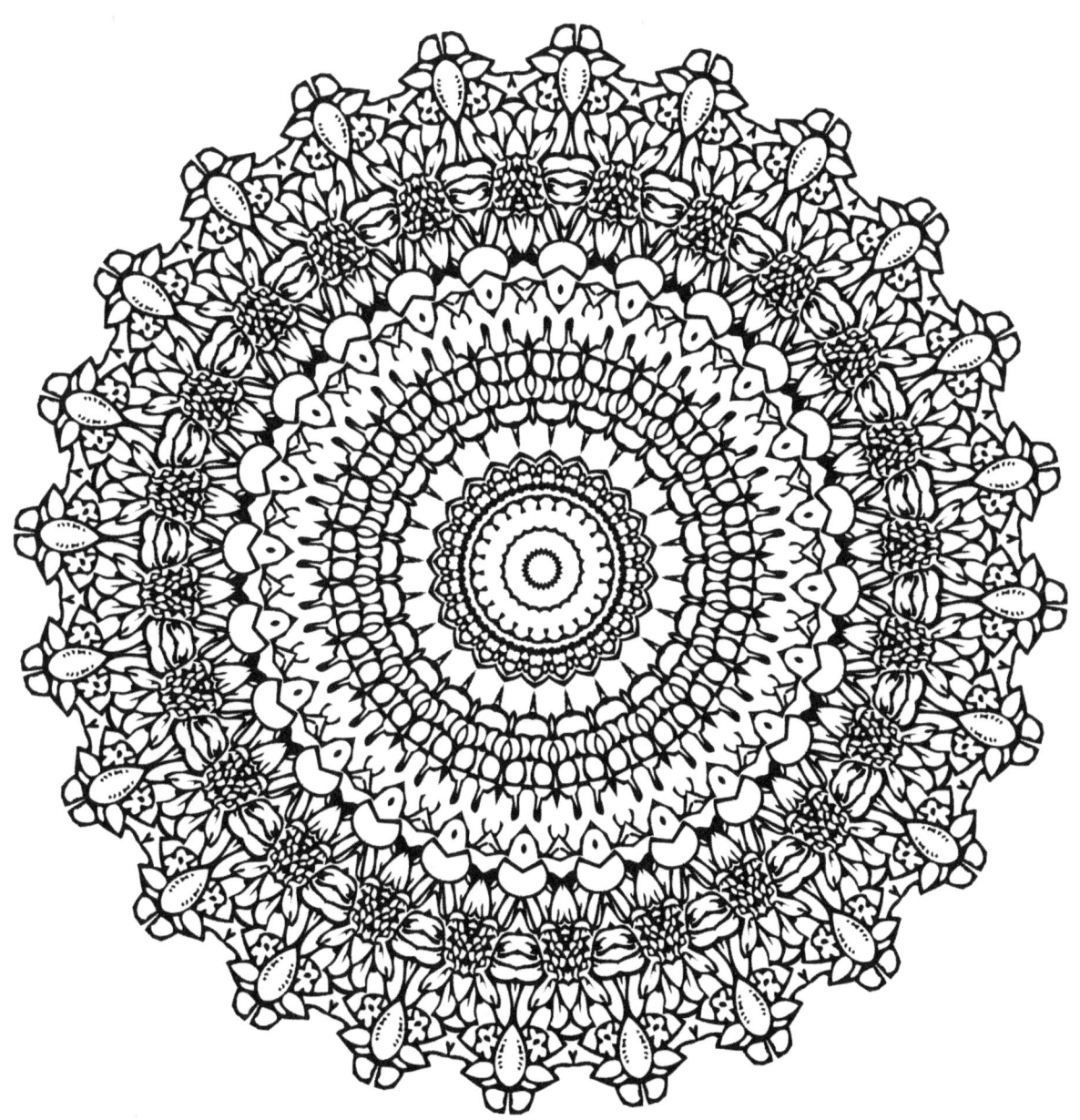

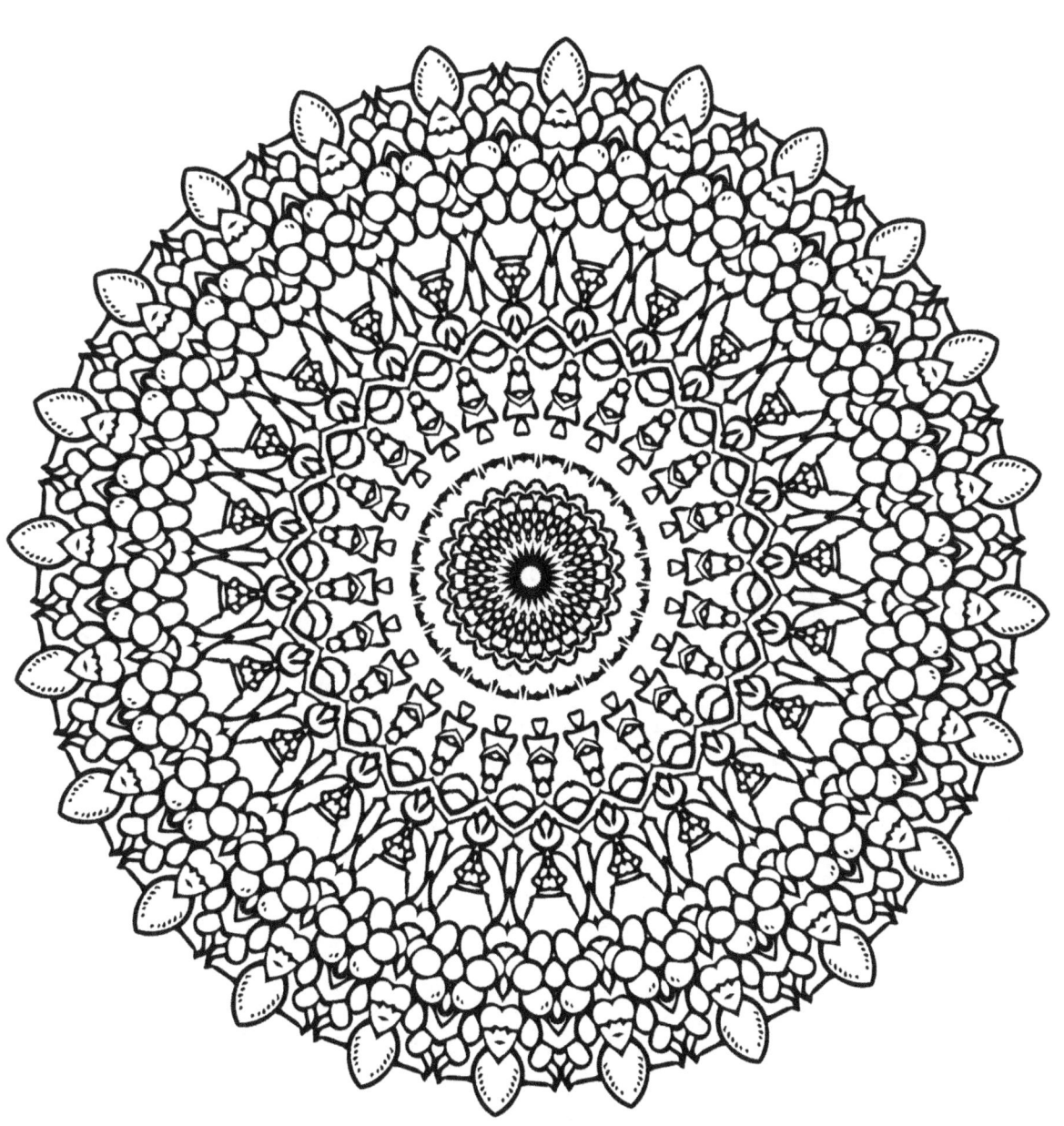

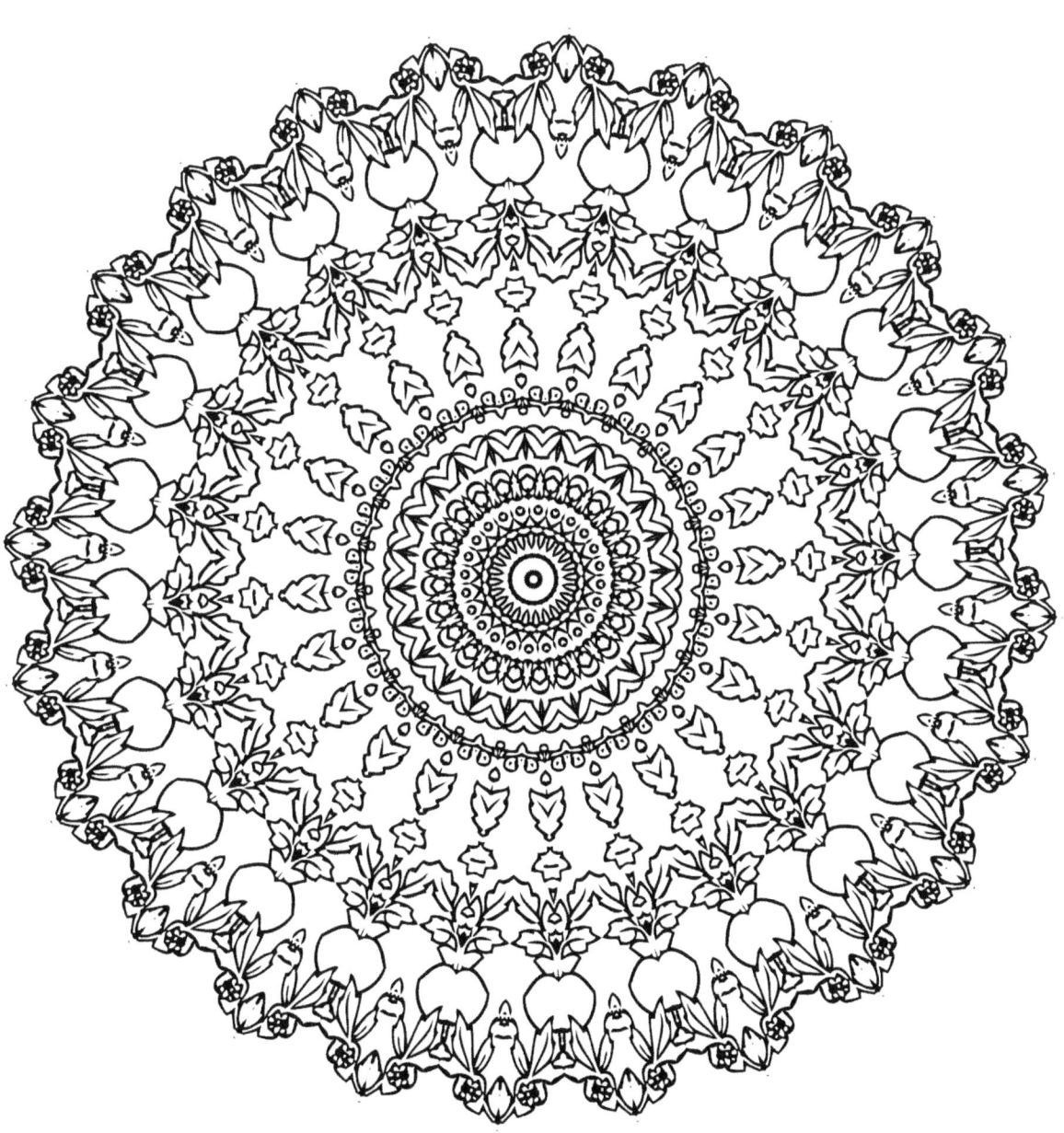

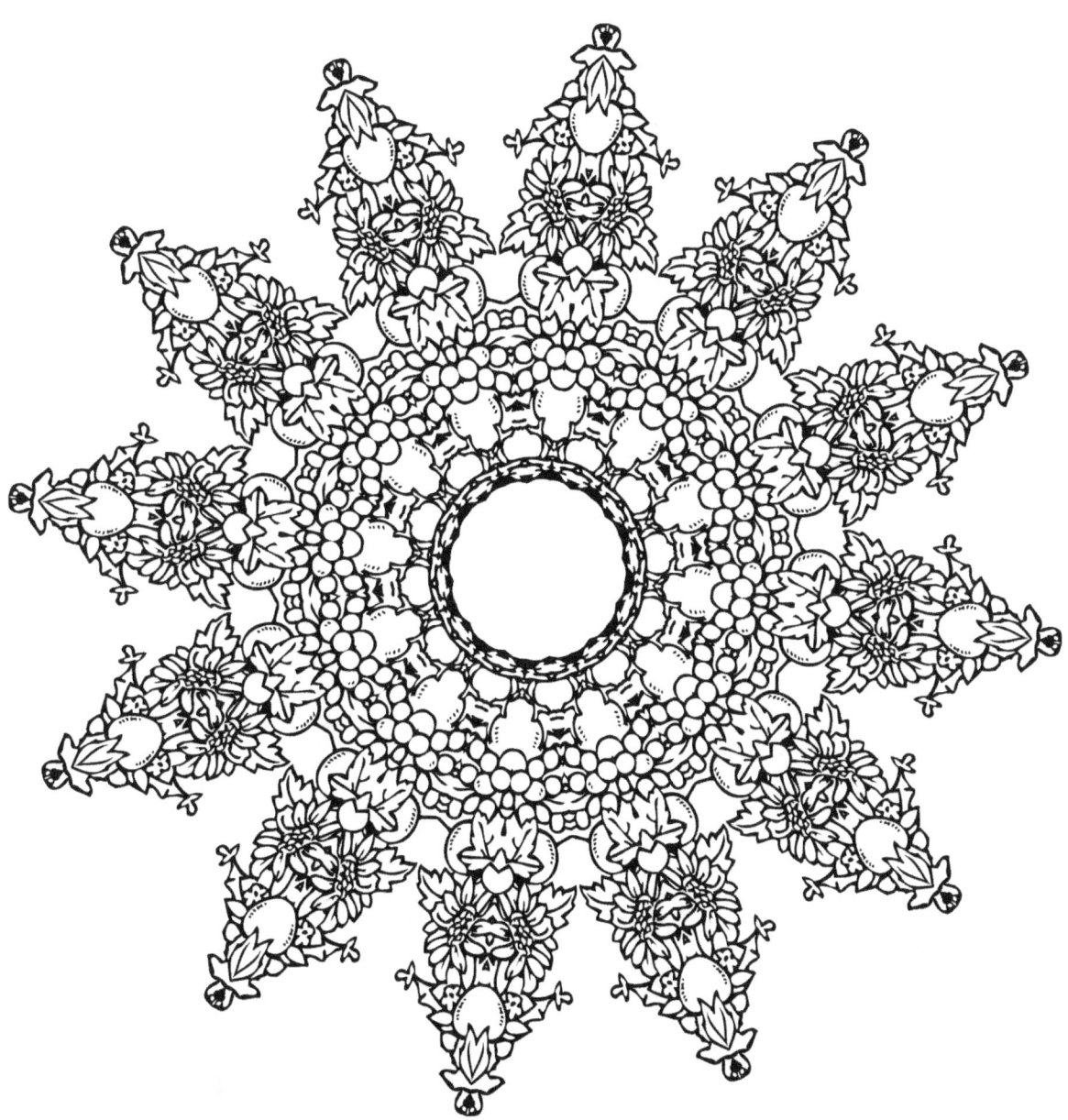

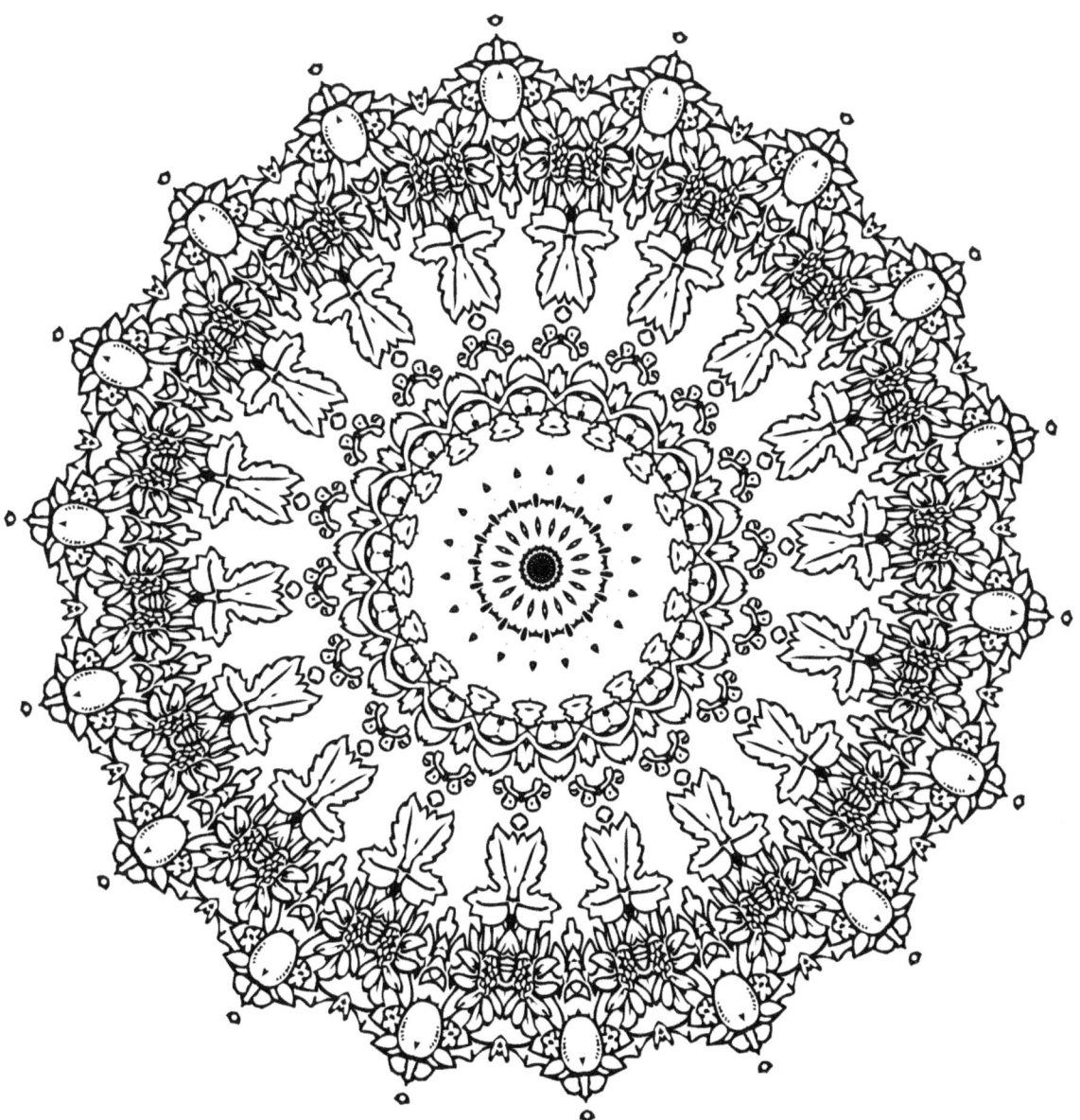

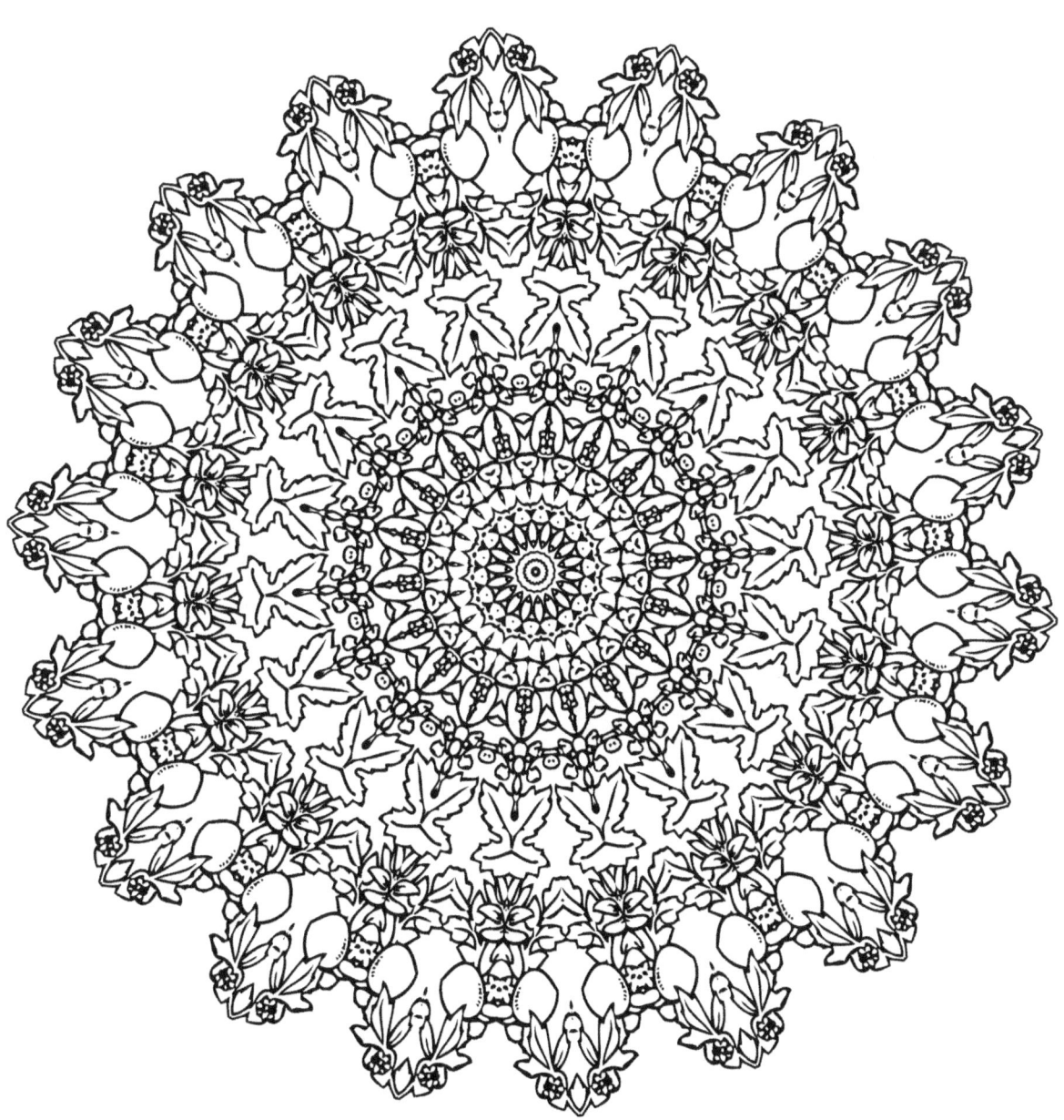

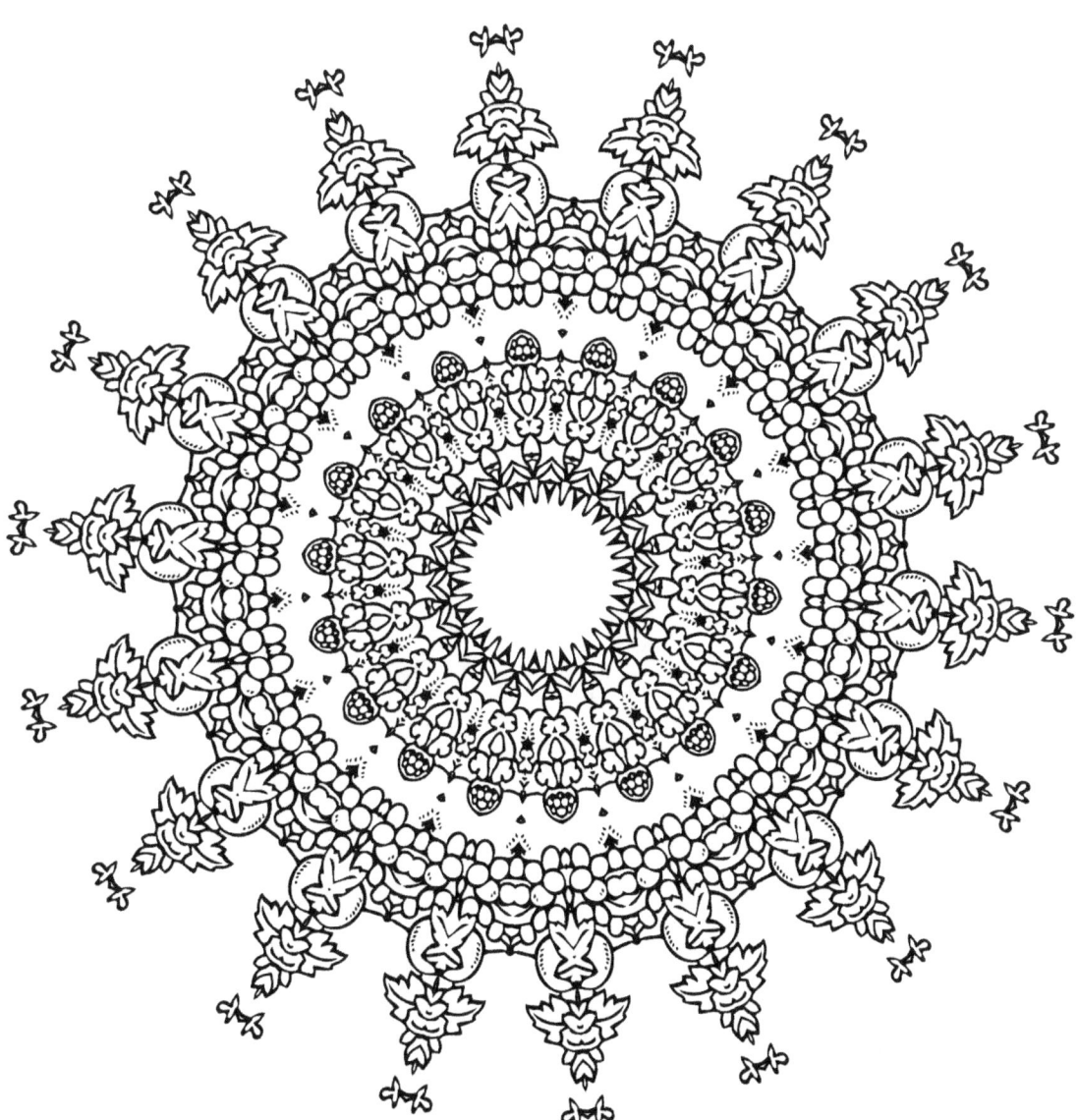

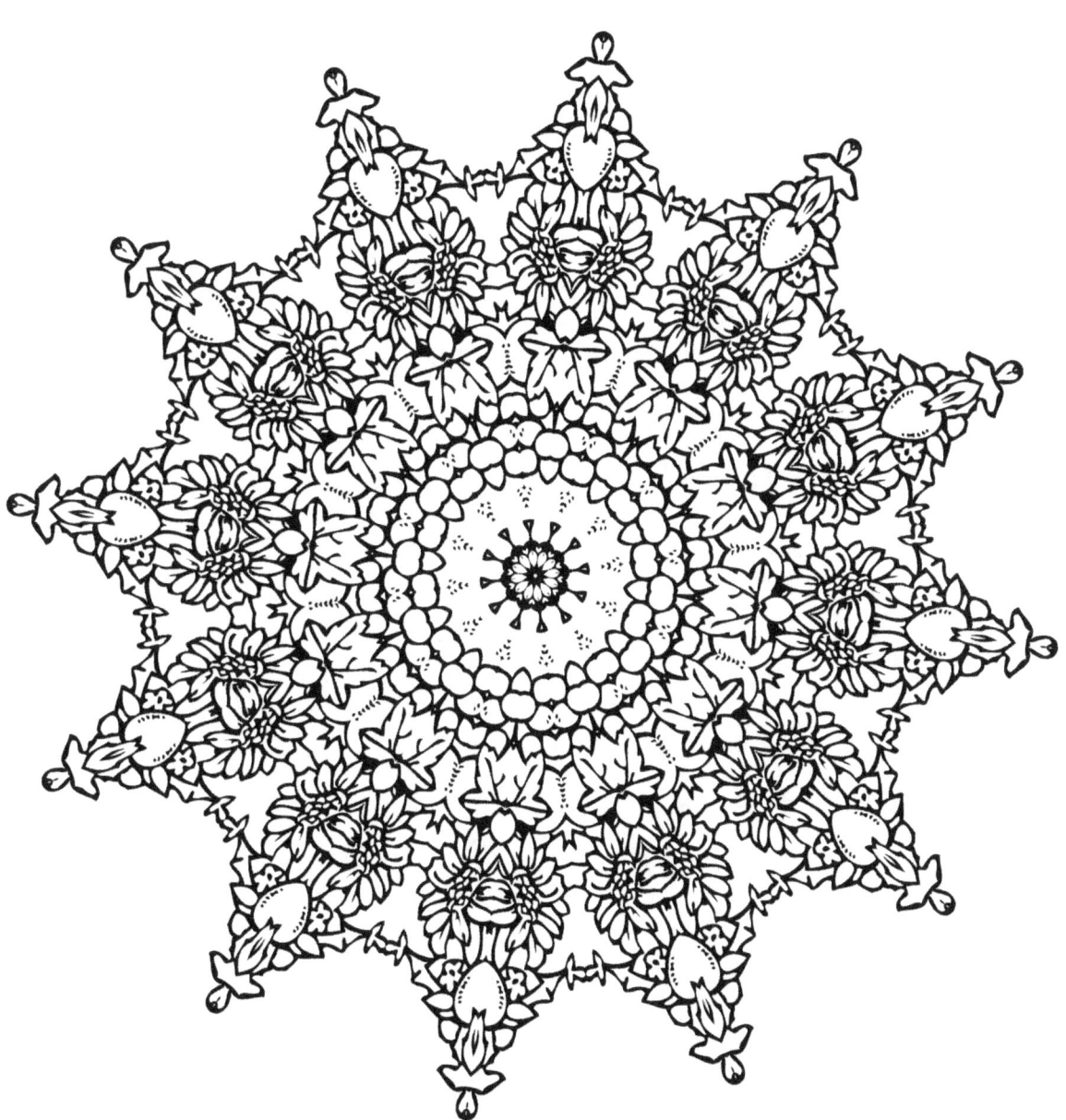

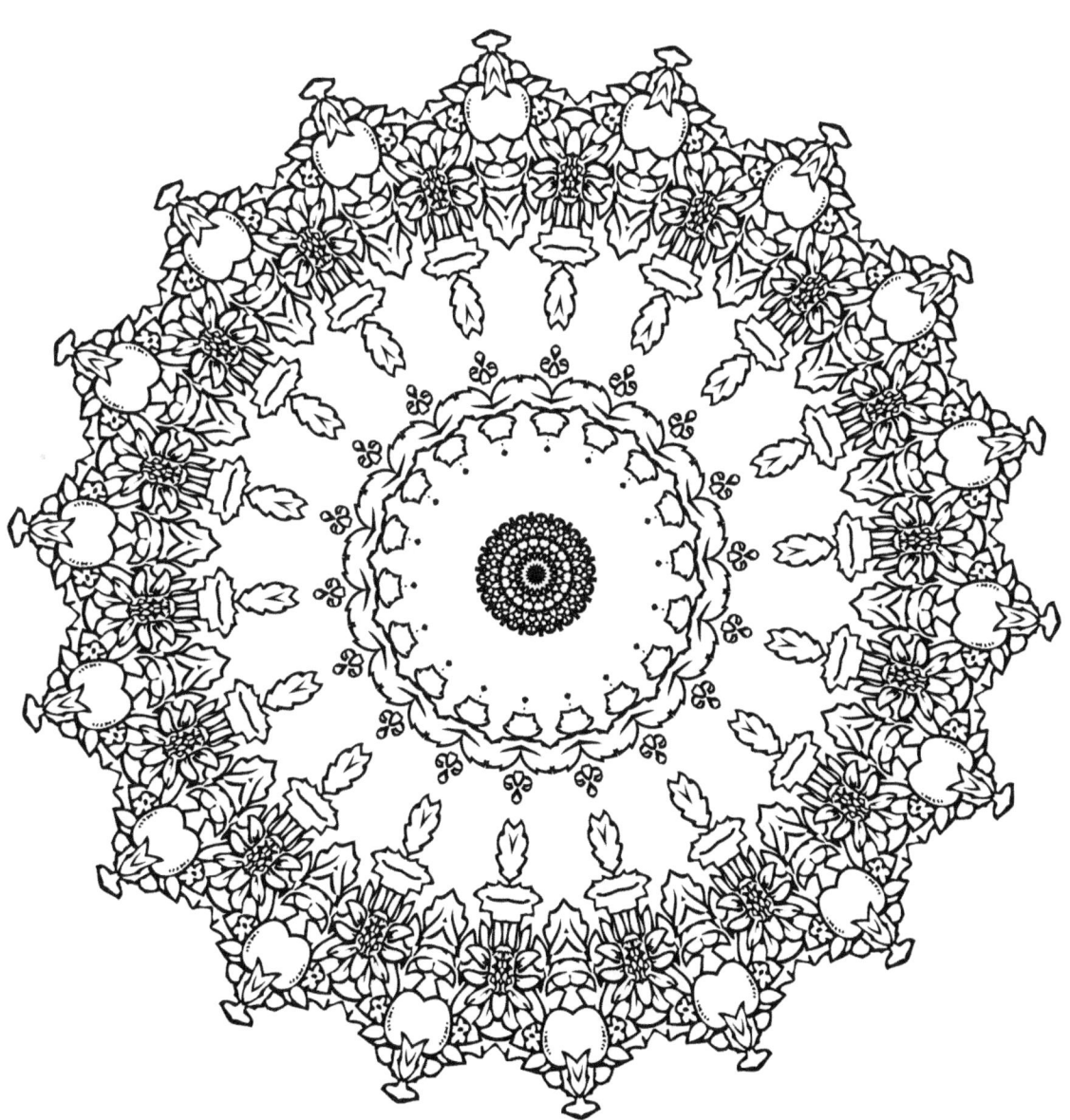

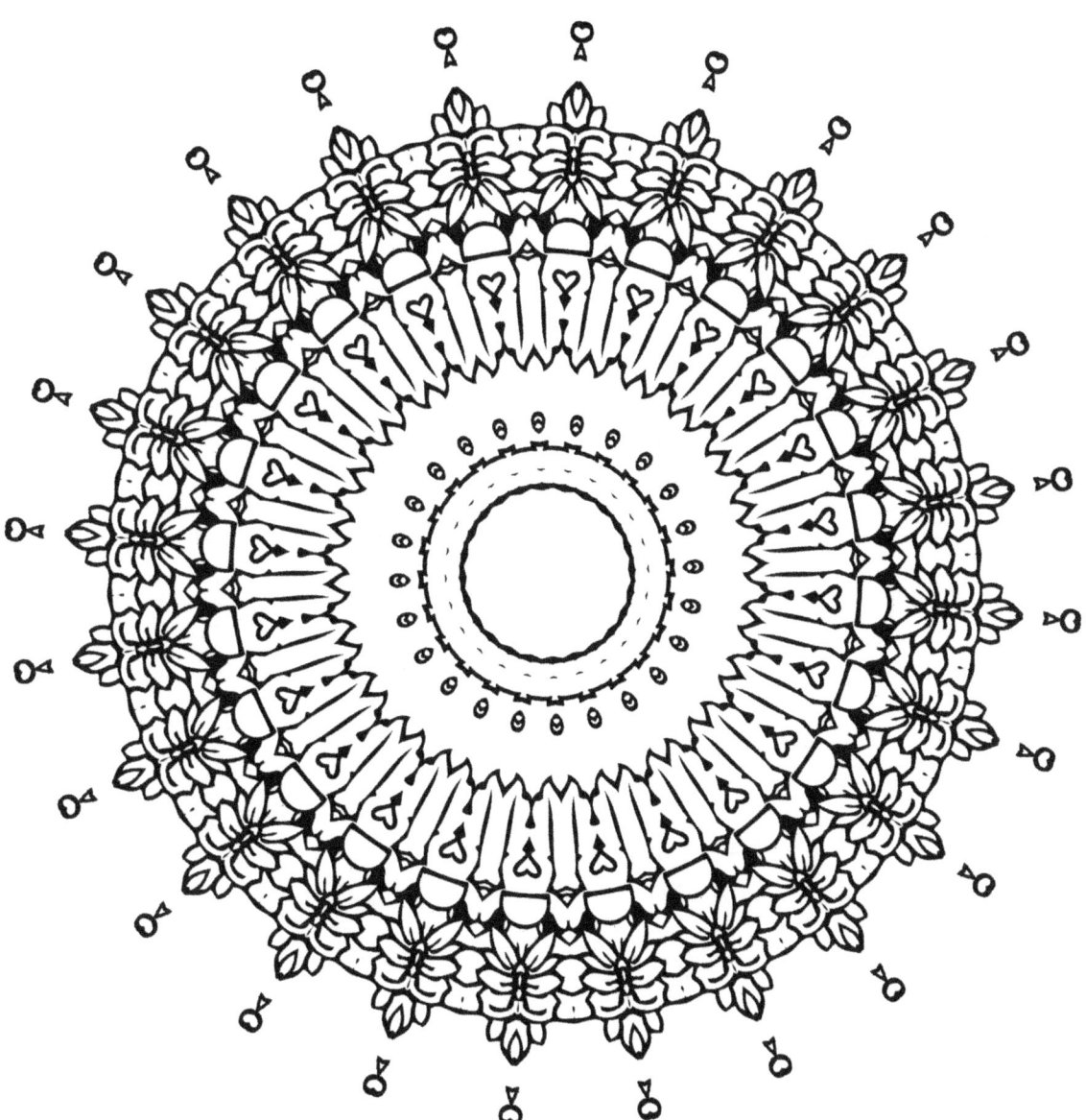

FINAL WORD

Thank you for your purchase!

More coloring books coming soon from Art Therapy Designs.

See our Facebook page for updates and giveaways!

Visit: www.facebook.com/ArtTherapyDesigns